Violence in the Media

Other Books in the Current Controversies Series

Assisted Suicide

Developing Nations

E-books

Family Violence

Gays in the Military

Global Warming

Human Trafficking

The Iranian Green Movement

Jobs in America

Medical Ethics

Modern-Day Piracy

Pakistan

Politics and Religion

Pollution

Rap and Hip-Hop

Vaccines

Women in Politics

CURRENT CONTROVERSIES

Violence in the Media

Dedria Bryfonski, Book Editor

GREENHAVEN PRESS
A part of Gale, Cengage Learning

GALE
CENGAGE Learning·

Detroit • New York • San Francisco • New Haven, Conn • Waterville, Maine • London

Elizabeth Des Chenes, *Director, Content Strategy*
Cynthia Sanner, *Publisher*
Douglas Dentino, *Manager, New Product*

© 2014 Greenhaven Press, a part of Gale, Cengage Learning

WCN: 01-100-101

Gale and Greenhaven Press are registered trademarks used herein under license.

For more information, contact:
Greenhaven Press
27500 Drake Rd.
Farmington Hills, MI 48331-3535
Or you can visit our Internet site at gale.cengage.com

For product information and technology assistance, contact us at

Gale Customer Support, 1-800-877-4253
For permission to use material from this text or product, submit all requests online at
www.cengage.com/permissions

Further permissions questions can be emailed to permissionrequest@cengage.com

Articles in Greenhaven Press anthologies are often edited for length to meet page requirements. In addition, original titles of these works are changed to clearly present the main thesis and to explicitly indicate the author's opinion. Every effort is made to ensure that Greenhaven Press accurately reflects the original intent of the authors. Every effort has been made to trace the owners of copyrighted material.

Cover image copyright © Photothek/Andia/Alamy.

LIBRARY OF CONGRESS CATALOGING-IN-PUBLICATION DATA

Violence in the media / Dedria Bryfonski, book editor.
    p. cm. -- (Current controversies)
    Includes bibliographical references and index.
    ISBN 978-0-7377-3299-3 (hardcover) -- ISBN 978-0-7377-3300-6 (pbk.)
    1. Violence in mass media. I. Bryfonski, Dedria.
    P96.V5V54 2014
    303.6--dc23

2013028044

Printed in the United States of America
1 2 3 4 5 6 7 18 17 16 15 14

Contents

Foreword   13

Introduction   16

Chapter 1: Are Violent Music Lyrics and Videos Harmful?

Overview: The Relationship Between Rap   21
Music and Violence Is Complex

Mark Asbridge, Julian Tanner, and Scot Wortley

A study of a large sample of Toronto students revealed more delinquent behavior among fans of rap music than their counterparts. However, there were marked racial differences in these findings. Asian and white teens who listened to rap music were more likely to be involved in criminal behavior than their peers, while black fans of rap music were no more likely to engage in criminal behavior than black teens who were not fans of rap music.

Yes: Violent Music Lyrics and Videos Are Harmful

There Is a Link Between Violent Lyrics   30
and Violent Behavior

Matthew Robinson

Studies show that children and teenagers who listen to rap and hip-hop music are more apt to commit violent acts and abuse alcohol. Normal kids usually aren't at risk, but teens dealing with behavioral issues can be negatively affected by violent music.

Music Videos Glorifying Violence Send   33
the Wrong Message

Parents Television Council

The pop star Rihanna's video "Man Down," showing her shooting and killing the man who raped her, sends a terrible message to rape victims. Instead of urging victims to seek help, this video condones retaliation in the form of murder.

No: Violent Music Lyrics and Videos Are Not Harmful to Children and Teens

Listening to Rap Music Does Not Make
Teens Violent   36

Jennifer Copley

There have been a variety of studies on a possible link
between rap music and violence, but not one conclusively shows that rap music fosters violence in children
and teens. However, it may be that teens at-risk for violence are also attracted to rap music.

Violence in Music Videos Mirrors Violence   42
in Society

Gil Kaufman

Defending the video in which she guns down her rapist,
Rihanna argues that teenagers need to be exposed to reality, or they'll never learn to adapt.

Chapter 2: Is Exposure to Violence in Television and Movies Harmful?

Violent Youth: The Censoring and   46
Public Reception of *The Wild One*
and *The Blackboard Jungle*

Jerold Simmons

Violence in the movies has been a concern of movie censors since the early 1930s. Two successful films of the
1950s, *The Wild One* and *The Blackboard Jungle*, were
highly controversial for the violence they portrayed,
bringing the issue of film violence to a new level of interest, even prompting hearings in the US Senate. And
while the movie studios feared the government might
censor their films, they actually expanded the role of violence in them as a way to increase revenues.

**Yes: Exposure to Violence in Television
and Movies Is Harmful**

Violence on Television Can Contribute   70
to Aggressive Behavior

Kyla Boyse

Research conclusively makes the link between exposure to media violence and violent behavior. Media violence contributes to aggressive behavior in children and desensitizes them to violence.

The Combination of Humor and Violence in Television Advertising Is Increasing
Benjamin J. Blackford et al.

75

A study of Super Bowl ads since 2005 showing that viewers favor television advertising that combines violence and humor is troubling because the combination of the two, researchers believe, desensitizes people to violence. Of even more concern, the number of these types of ads has increased significantly since 2005.

Exposure to Media Violence Increases Aggressive and Violent Behavior
Craig A. Anderson and Soledad Liliana Escobar-Chaves

83

As children and teenagers spend more and more time using various forms of electronic media, they are exposed to increasing amounts of violence. Media violence has been conclusively shown to increase the likelihood of aggressive and violent behavior in both children and teenagers. In fact, the causal link between media violence and later violent behavior is greater than that between such behavior and substance abuse, poverty, abusive parents, or having a low IQ.

Watching Violent Movies Encourages Teenagers to Drink Alcohol
Society for Prevention Research

89

Teenagers who watch R-rated movies are more likely to try alcohol at an earlier age. In addition, watching R-rated movies makes teens more likely to engage in risky behavior, including alcohol abuse.

No: Exposure to Violence in Television and Movies Is Not Harmful

Taming Baby Rage: Why Are Some Kids So Angry?
Nikhil Swaminathan

92

Research has shown that violent behavior begins in children long before they are exposed to television and other violent media. The cause of violence in children can be traced to their genetic make-up—children with damaged genes have greater difficulty learning, which can cause frustration that can lead to violent behavior.

Violence in the Media Has No Negative Effect on the General Population   95

Tom Grimes, James A. Anderson, and Lori Bergen

The theories postulated to explain the connection between violence in the media and violent behavior are simply not compatible with the social science theories that explain human behavior. While violence in the media may have a negative effect on psychologically unwell people, it does not have the same effect on the general population.

The Research Linking Media Violence to Aggression Is Weak and Ambiguous   100

Free Expression Policy Project

The research linking media violence to aggression or crime is inconsistent and weak. According to the US Supreme Court in their ruling striking down a law restricting minor's access to video games, "most of the studies suffer from significant, admitted flaws in methodology."

Chapter 3: Are Violent Video Games Harmful?

Overview: There Are Benefits as Well as Dangers from Video Games   106

Bill Jenkins

Both proponents and detractors of video games are correct in their assessment of the potential effects video games can have. There is evidence that video games affect and change the brain for both good and bad. Factors, such as time spent playing video games, game mechanics and context, impact whether the video games have a negative or positive impact.

The Demise of Guys': How Video Games and Porn Are Ruining a Generation   109

Philip G. Zimbardo and Nikita Duncan

More and more young men are getting addicted to the high they get from video games and online pornography. This could have negative consequences for society as young men are trading the reality of relationships, school, and jobs for the constant thrills they get online.

Violent Video Games Change   113
Young Men's Brainwaves

Rupert Shepherd

Researchers used functional magnetic resonance imaging to determine that playing violent video games has a long-term effect on the brains of young men, negatively impacting the portions of the brain associated with cognitive function and emotional control.

Violent Video Games Influence   116
Children to Kill

Flare

Violent video games are sending children the message that killing someone is acceptable behavior. While violent video games are not the only reason for the escalation of violence in the world, because these games desensitize children to the effects of violence, they are a contributing factor.

No: Violent Video Games Are Not Harmful

The Dubious Perils of Pac-Man   119

Timothy Maher

There is no research supporting the claims of former US surgeon general C. Everett Koop and others that video games make children more violent. Video games have educational purposes and do more good than harm.

Athwart: To Save the Dead-Eyed Child?   122

James Lileks

The US Supreme Court was right to strike down a California law that banned the sale of violent video games to minors. Most video games are harmless and it is easy enough for parents to identify which games they don't want their children to play. The decision to limit access to violent video games should be the responsibility of parents and individuals, not government.

Research Reporting Adverse Effects   **126**
of Violent Video Games Is Flawed and
Possibly Biased

John Walker

A study that concludes that violent video games have an effect on the brain is suspect for two reasons. First, while the study showed changes in brain waves, it did not show that the subjects exhibited any violent behavior. Second, the study was funded by the Center for Successful Parenting, which appears to be a parenting advocacy group with a stated bias against the sale of violent video games.

Chapter 4: How Should Society Respond to Violence in the Media?

Chapter Preface   **131**

Parents Need to Monitor Their Children's   **134**
Media Habits

Florence Cherry and Jo Ann Zenger

It is the job of parents, not the government, to monitor the amount and kind of television that their children view. Parents should be concerned about violence on television because exposure to violence can make children fearful or anxious or make them believe that violence is an acceptable behavior in the real world.

Advocacy Groups Play an Important Role   **139**
in Developing Media Policies for Children

Amy B. Jordan

The effectiveness of federal media regulations for children is limited because many media companies comply only with the letter of the law and find ways to circumvent it. Advocacy groups, who have no hidden agenda, are effective watchdogs for parents and children.

The Motion Picture Production Code Is   **144**
Effective in Restricting Movie Violence

Joel Timmer

Although there had been little research on the effects of violence in the media in the late 1920s when the Motion Picture Production Code was created, current research shows that the framers did amazingly well in identifying and restricting the types of violence most harmful to viewers.

Movie Ratings Are an Ineffective Form of Censorship   158

Nicholas Ransbottom

The problem with movie ratings and censorship as a whole is that people have different reactions to the same thing and find different things offensive and disturbing. Additionally, ratings undermine the art of making movies because they can potentially alter or censor forms of expression that some may find offensive.

Organizations to Contact   160

Bibliography   166

Index   171

Foreword

By definition, controversies are "discussions of questions in which opposing opinions clash" (*Webster's Twentieth Century Dictionary Unabridged*). Few would deny that controversies are a pervasive part of the human condition and exist on virtually every level of human enterprise. Controversies transpire between individuals and among groups, within nations and between nations. Controversies supply the grist necessary for progress by providing challenges and challengers to the status quo. They also create atmospheres where strife and warfare can flourish. A world without controversies would be a peaceful world; but it also would be, by and large, static and prosaic.

The Series' Purpose

The purpose of the Current Controversies series is to explore many of the social, political, and economic controversies dominating the national and international scenes today. Titles selected for inclusion in the series are highly focused and specific. For example, from the larger category of criminal justice, Current Controversies deals with specific topics such as police brutality, gun control, white collar crime, and others. The debates in Current Controversies also are presented in a useful, timeless fashion. Articles and book excerpts included in each title are selected if they contribute valuable, long-range ideas to the overall debate. And wherever possible, current information is enhanced with historical documents and other relevant materials. Thus, while individual titles are current in focus, every effort is made to ensure that they will not become quickly outdated. Books in the Current Controversies series will remain important resources for librarians, teachers, and students for many years.

In addition to keeping the titles focused and specific, great care is taken in the editorial format of each book in the series. Book introductions and chapter prefaces are offered to provide background material for readers. Chapters are organized around several key questions that are answered with diverse opinions representing all points on the political spectrum. Materials in each chapter include opinions in which authors clearly disagree as well as alternative opinions in which authors may agree on a broader issue but disagree on the possible solutions. In this way, the content of each volume in Current Controversies mirrors the mosaic of opinions encountered in society. Readers will quickly realize that there are many viable answers to these complex issues. By questioning each author's conclusions, students and casual readers can begin to develop the critical thinking skills so important to evaluating opinionated material.

Current Controversies is also ideal for controlled research. Each anthology in the series is composed of primary sources taken from a wide gamut of informational categories including periodicals, newspapers, books, US and foreign government documents, and the publications of private and public organizations. Readers will find factual support for reports, debates, and research papers covering all areas of important issues. In addition, an annotated table of contents, an index, a book and periodical bibliography, and a list of organizations to contact are included in each book to expedite further research.

Perhaps more than ever before in history, people are confronted with diverse and contradictory information. During the Persian Gulf War, for example, the public was not only treated to minute-to-minute coverage of the war, it was also inundated with critiques of the coverage and countless analyses of the factors motivating US involvement. Being able to sort through the plethora of opinions accompanying today's major issues, and to draw one's own conclusions, can be a complicated and frustrating struggle. It is the editors' hope that Current Controversies will help readers with this struggle.

Introduction

"The advent of each new form of media has brought with it a concern that the violence reflected in it could encourage violent behavior in society."

The debate over the impact of violent content goes back to classical times. Greek philosopher Plato argued in *The Republic* for censorship of the media, saying, "The young can't distinguish what is allegorical from what isn't, and the opinions they absorb at that age are hard to erase and apt to become unalterable." Plato's disciple Aristotle had the opposite view, contending in his *Poetics* and *Politics* that the violence in tragic plays has a cathartic effect on people and is an effective way of purging negative emotions.

Since that time, the advent of each new form of media has brought with it a concern that the violence reflected in it could encourage violent behavior in society. In the nineteenth century, moralists cautioned that newspaper stories about violent acts would encourage people to mimic that behavior. Concerns about the impact of violence in the movies began in the 1920s and led to the Payne Fund Studies in 1933–35, which concluded that the violence in film was a direct cause of young people becoming criminals and delinquents. The ubiquity of television in American households in the 1950s and 1960s gave rise to increasing concern about the impact that violent programming had on children. US Senate subcommittees in 1954 and again in 1961 and 1962 examined the impact of television violence. Considerable research has been done on the topic, notably a study published in 1961 by Wilbur Schramm, Jack Lyle, and Edwin B. Parker titled *Television in the Lives of Our Children*, which concluded:

"For *some* children, under *some* conditions, *some* television is harmful. For *other* children, under the same conditions, or for the same children under *other* conditions, it may be beneficial. For *most* children, under *most* conditions, *most* television is probably neither harmful nor particularly beneficial."

Citing studies conducted in 1969 and 1982, the American Psychological Association identifies three major effects of seeing violence on television: children may become less sensitive to the pain and suffering of others; children may become more fearful; and children are more likely to imitate aggressive behavior.

Video games are a more recent technology, and thus research on the effects of violence in video games is less complete. However, concerns about the effects of violence started in 1976 and focused on *Death Race*, an arcade game. In 1993, *Mortal Kombat* and *Night Trap* stirred such a controversy that a US Senate hearing was held to debate federal video game regulations.

The popularity of rap and hip-hop music beginning in the 1990s led to a new concern—the impact of violent music lyrics. The most widely cited study was done in 2003 by psychologist Craig A. Anderson, whose research concluded that songs with violent lyrics increased aggression-related thoughts.

Debate about a potential link between violent media and violent behavior is sparked whenever there is a well-publicized violent incident where the perpetrator claimed to be influenced by a form of violent media. Examples abound. John Hinckley, who attempted to assassinate President Ronald Reagan, was reportedly obsessed with the movie *Taxi Driver*. Mass murderer Charles Manson claimed his actions were inspired by the lyrics in the Beatles' song "Helter Skelter." Columbine High School shooters Eric Harris and Dylan Klebold were allegedly addicted to the video game *Doom* and became frustrated when their parents took away their gaming privileges.

On July 20, 2012, James Holmes, dressed to resemble the character "the Joker" in the movie *The Dark Knight Rises*, opened fire in a theater showing the film, killing twelve people and wounding fifty-eight, police said. Once again, commentators debated whether exposure to violent media played a role in the tragedy.

Media scholar David Zurawik discounts the notion that violence in the media is to blame, citing all of the people who are exposed to violent acts on television and the movies and who don't kill others. "In 30 years of writing about and studying the media, and 20 years of teaching it, I absolutely believe you cannot blame the movies for Holmes' alleged act unless you want to discard the evidence and research by media scholars," Zurawik is quoted by Nsenga K. Burton in *The Root*.

Also arguing that the media is not to blame, Anthony Lane in "A Shooting in a Movie Theater," appearing in the *New Yorker*, said:

> "[No] film makes you kill. Having a mind to kill, at least in any systematic fashion, means that your mind is ready-warped; that the warping may well have started long before, perhaps in childhood; and that you may perhaps seek out, or be drawn to, areas of sensation—notably those entailing sex or violence—which can encourage, inflame, or accelerate the warping."

Taking the opposing view was Dana Stevens in "Why There?" which appeared in the online magazine *Slate*:

> I can't get away from the fact that this act of violence took place—with, from the look of it, considerable advance planning—at an opening-night midnight showing of *The Dark Knight Rises*, a movie that . . . envisions modernity as a lawless dystopia where just such a thing might happen. . . . [Di-

rector Christopher] Nolan's Batman trilogy has proceeded on the assumption that what happens on the screen in some way reflects on what's happening in the world, that fantasy and reality are mutually permeable—this is what makes his movies function as political allegories, if at times muddled ones. Why shouldn't we assume the reverse is true as well—that the grim, violent fantasies we gather to consume as a culture have some power to bleed over from the screen into real life?

The impact of violence in the media continues to be hotly debated. In *Current Controversies: Violence in the Media* the controversies surrounding this topic are debated in the following chapters: Are Violent Music Lyrics and Videos Harmful? Is Exposure to Violence in Television and Movies Harmful? Are Violent Video Games Harmful? and How Should Society Respond to Violence in the Media?

CHAPTER 1

Are Violent Music Lyrics and Videos Harmful?

Overview: The Relationship Between Rap Music and Violence Is Complex

Mark Asbridge, Julian Tanner, and Scot Wortley

Mark Asbridge is an associate professor of education at the University of Toronto; Julian Tanner is a professor in the department of social sciences at the University of Toronto; and Scot Wortley is a an associate professor of criminology at the University of Toronto.

The emergence and spectacular growth of rap is probably the most important development in popular music since the rise of rock 'n' roll in the late 1940s. Radio airplay, music video programming and sales figures are obvious testimonies to its popularity and commercial success. This was made particularly evident in October 2003 when, according to the recording industry bible *Billboard* magazine, all top 10 acts in the United States were rap or hip-hop artists; and again in 2006, when the Academy award for Best Song went to "It's Hard Out Here for a Pimp," a rap song by the group Three 6 Mafia.

Such developments may also signal rap's increasing social acceptance and cultural legitimization. However, its reputation and status in the musical field has, hitherto, been a controversial one. Like new music before it (jazz, rock 'n' roll), rap has been critically reviewed as a corrosive influence on young and impressionable listeners. Whether rap has been reviled as much as jazz and rock 'n' roll once were is a moot point; rather more certain is its pre-eminent role as a problematic contemporary musical genre. . . .

Mark Asbridge, Julian Tanner, and Scot Wortley, "Listening to Rap: Cultures of Crime, Cultures of Resistance," *Social Forces*, Vol. 88, No. 2, December 2009, p. 693, by permission of Oxford University Press.

Researchers Are Divided on the Effects of Rap

Much of the early work on audiences preoccupied itself with investigating the harmful effects of media exposure, especially the effects of depictions of violence in movies and TV on real life criminal events. Results have generally been inconclusive, with considerable disagreement in the social science research community regarding the influence of the media on those watching the large or small screen.

Listening to popular music has, on occasion, been said to produce similarly negative effects, although these too have proven difficult to verify. For example, in one high profile case in the 1980s, the heavy metal band Judas Priest was accused of producing recorded material (songs) that contained subliminal messaging that led to the suicides of two fans. This claim was not, however, legally validated because the judge hearing the case remained unconvinced about a causal linkage between the music and the self-destructive behavior of two individuals. . . .

The idea that exposure to rap music causes crime is not unequivocally supported in the research literature.

The search for the harmful effects of rap music has yielded no more definitive results than earlier quests for media effects. While some studies report evidence of increased violence, delinquency, substance use, and unsafe sexual activity resulting from young people's exposure to rap music, other researchers have failed to find such a link or have exercised extreme caution when interpreting apparent links. One review of the literature, conducted in the 1990s, could find a total of only nine investigations—all of them small-scale, none involving the general adolescent population—and concluded that there was an even split between those that found some sort of an association between exposure to the music and various deviant or undesirable outcomes, and those that could find no connection at all. Moreover, in those studies where the music and the wrongdoing were linked, investigators were very circumspect about whether or not they were observing a causal relationship, and if so, which came first, the music or the violent dispositions. . . .

The Present Study Examines How Rap Is Used in Everyday Life

The present study is concerned with three key questions: First, is there a relationship between audiences for rap and representations of the music? Second, as compared to other listening audiences, are serious rap fans participants in cultures of crime and resistance? Third, if such a link is found, what are the sources of variation in their participation in these cultures of crime and resistance? . . .

Whereas most contemporary research on rap focuses on those who create the music—artists and producers, and those who write about it, music critics—we pose questions about rap's audience. Further, while audience studies usually employ qualitative data-gathering techniques, we use the methods of survey research.

We are more concerned with how audience members interact with the music than with the issue of cause and effect. We are interested in how music might be used as a resource in their everyday lives, how it might contribute to identity formation and, especially, how audiences might align themselves with (or distance themselves from) cultures of crime and resistance. Nonetheless, in our analyses, we treat rap fandom as a dependent variable. While there is considerable academic and public debate about whether music produces or is a product of cultural activities, legal or otherwise, existing research has failed to provide a compelling or consistent rationale for any particular causal logic. As we have seen, the idea that exposure to rap music causes crime is not unequivocally supported in the research literature. Research on resistant youth cultures, by contrast, is much more likely to reverse the relationship and see musical style as a result of subcultural activity. [Dick] Hebdige, for example, infers that punk rock in the United Kingdom was a cultural response to the subordination of existing working-class youth groups. [Dave] Laing has countered that punk the musical genre existed before punk the subculture. In the absence of agreement about the direction of the relationship between musical taste and cultural practices, our decision to operationalize rap appreciation as a dependent variable is made more for pragmatic, heuristic [problem-solving by experimental methods] reasons than unassailable theoretical ones.

Our strategy is to focus on listening preferences rather than purchasing habits. By asking students to report on and evaluate the music that they like, dislike and in what combinations, we gain a clearer and more detailed picture of where rap is situated in the consumption patterns of groups of students differentiated by, among other factors, their racial identity. Our goals are to: 1). distinguish students with a serious, exclusive taste for rap from more casual fans; 2). to calculate the size and racial makeup of rap music's prime audience; and 3). to map relationships between that core audience and resistant and delinquent repertoires.

Few surveys of general populations of young people have established any kind of connection between rap and deviancy, net of other factors. We contend that rap's reputation as a corrosive force is validated by that linkage, and that without it that representation becomes more contestable. A similar logic applies to the relationship between rap and social protest. The claim that the music carries a serious message—that it is an expression of resistant values and perceptions—is substantiated with evidence of a link between the music and a collective sense of inequity, and weakened by its absence. . . .

Rap Is Enormously Popular

We can quickly confirm the enormous popularity of rap with our respondents. It has the highest average approval rating of any musical genre, with some 35 percent of students saying that they liked it "very much," and 21 percent saying that they liked it "quite a lot." Rap clearly appeals to a broad range of young listeners and is, therefore very much part of a common music culture among high school students. But our cluster analysis also isolates a group of students who enjoy rap music and little else. Examining the approval rating for each music genre relative to the cluster means, where scores approaching 1 indicate a strong approval of the genre, and scores approaching 5 indicate a strong dislike, demonstrates that Urban Music Enthusiasts have a strong preference for rap and hip-hop, reggae and dance hall; a more moderate liking for soul and R&B, and a below average liking for all other musical genres.

> *What is common to . . . Urban Music Enthusiasts is that, compared to other students in our sample, they are poorly endowed with cultural capital and are not especially good students.*

We think that our Urban Music Enthusiasts [teens who like rap and hip hop and are not interested in other musical styles] fit the profile of music univores—individuals who appreciate a few musical styles while disliking everything else—as described in the research of [Richard A.] Peterson and [Bethany] Bryson. Bryson links univorous taste among American adults to low status, particular racial and ethnic groups, and regional differences. She also notes that univorous taste, when compared to omnivorous taste, is more likely to be related to what she calls "sub-cultural spheres."

Our Urban Music Enthusiasts appear to be rap univores who may also be adhering to "sub-cultural spheres." Of the 605 Urban Music Enthusiasts in our sample, 275 (46%) are black, 117 (19%) are white, 115 (19%) are Asian or South Asian, and 98 (16%) are from other racial groups. These figures tell us that young black people still comprise the central component of the rap audience; moreover, roughly 57 percent of black youth are Urban Music Enthusiasts. At the same time, we observe evidence of a significant racial crossover. White Urban Music Enthusiasts constitute 8.6 percent of the white students in our sample, while Asian Urban Music Enthusiasts make up 9.5 percent of all Asian students. The racial composition of the Urban Music Enthusiast taste culture prompts two further questions: First, of the black students surveyed, what factors in addition to race predict their univorous interest in rap? Second, of white and Asian students, what factors encourage their involvement in an essentially black music culture, an involvement that clearly sets them apart from other white and Asian students? . . .

Paying particular attention to the findings for each racial group, what is common to all three groups of Urban Music Enthusiasts is that, compared to other students in our sample, they are poorly endowed with cultural capital and are not especially good students. Few other background factors have any significant or consistent impact upon a disposition towards Urban Music. For white students, parental SES [socioeconomic status], family structure and subjective social class, have no bearing upon their musical preferences, whereas school suspension and poor grades are strong predictors. For black students, Urban Music enthusiasm is more common among younger students and those less likely to identify as Canadian. Being a black youth identified as an Urban Music Enthusiast is also strongly related to growing up in a single-parent family and skipping school. For their part, Asian/South Asian youth are something of an anomaly—among them, Urban Music Enthusiasm is positively associated with social class and having well-educated mothers—but like other Urban Music Enthusiasts it is also strongly related to school suspension and skipping school.

We are less interested, however, in the sociodemographic and socioeconomic factors that may lead to being an Urban Music Enthusiast than in the relationship between being a Urban Music Enthusiast and representations of rap—either as part of a culture of resistance and/or as a basis for subcultural delinquency. . . .

There Are Racial Variations in the Link Between Criminal Behavior and Rap

Our findings, with one notable exception, strongly confirm rap's reputation as protest music. Controlling for other factors, for both white and especially black youth, being an Urban Music Enthusiast is strongly related to feelings of social injustice. Indeed, for both these groups, a strong appreciation of rap is robustly and independently predicted by feelings of injustice, relative to the majority of remaining sociodemographic, socioeconomic class and school measures. Asian/South Asian youth are not part of this pattern. Feelings of injustice for Asian/South Asian youth is not connected to an appreciation of rap (though the direction of the effect is the same).

> *Among black youth—the largest constituency of Urban Music Enthusiasts—there is no relationship between involvement in either property crime or violent crime and rap music.*

If rap's reputation is enhanced when interpreted as protest music, it is correspondingly denigrated when linked to deviant behavior, particularly crimes of aggression and violence. Our findings suggest significant racial variations in the rap and crime relationships, and that overall, listening to rap is more strongly connected to property crime than to crimes of violence. . . .

Overall, property and violent crime demonstrate strong independent effects on listening to rap music. Individuals more involved in property crime and violent crime are more likely to be Urban Music Enthusiasts than individuals with little or no criminal involvement. However, race specific results offer an interesting twist. Involvement in property crime and violent crime is strongly related to an appreciation of rap music, net of other factors, among white and Asian/South Asian youth only. The group that does not fit this pattern is black youth, whose involvement in property and violent crime is not predictive of being an Urban Music Enthusiast. For black youth, an appreciation for rap music remains most strongly associated with feelings of social injustice, younger age and lower cultural capital. . . .

What our survey has also revealed . . . is that there are significant cross-cultural variations in how [rap] music is received.

The link between serious rap fandom and crime and delinquency is, however, considerably more equivocal and varied. Among black youth—the largest constituency of Urban Music Enthusiasts—there is no relationship between involvement in either property crime or violent crime and rap music. In other words, black youth, who pursue delinquent lifestyles, are no more likely to be core fans of rap than black youth who are uninvolved in crime. For core rap fans from the other two racial groups, a connection between crime and music is by and large confirmed: Asian/South Asian and, especially, white youth involved in property and violent crime are far more likely to be Urban Music Enthusiasts. How might we best interpret these findings?

Not causally, because like much of the existing research, ours is not a longitudinal [research conducted over a period of time] design. We are not, therefore, in any position to assign causality to the relationships that we have observed. White and Asian youth involved in criminal activity may have acquired their status as Urban Music Enthusiasts before they developed their criminal inclinations, not as a result of them; or earlier familial and educational experiences might have been responsible for both a taste for rap music and delinquent dispositions. Second, even if crime and rap fandom are causally linked among white and Asian youth, we still have to wrestle with the fact that there is no association between those variables among black Urban Music Enthusiasts (nor, of course, is there any association among those who listen to rap in conjunction with other musical genres). Although black youth commit their fair share of crime in Toronto [Canada], their criminality does not differentiate their musical preferences for rap compared to their more law-abiding peers.

These racial variations, nonetheless, encourage us to seriously doubt that subcultural delinquency has any straightforward impact on musical preferences, and to suspect that any explanation of them falls outside of the behaviorist dictates of cause and effect. . . .

Serious fans of rap music are different from other young music listeners—they are more inclined to crime and delinquency and more likely to subscribe to resistant attitudes and beliefs. Those familiar with popular representations of the music might have anticipated these findings; however, it has taken a survey to confirm the linkage between the music and cultures of crime and cultures of resistance. What our survey has also revealed—and what is not apparent from small-scale studies based on race specific samples—is that there are significant cross-cultural variations in how the music is received.

There Is a Link
Between Violent Lyrics
and Violent Behavior

Matthew Robinson

Matthew Robinson is a professor in the department of government and justice studies at Appalachian State University. He is president of the North Carolina Criminal Justice Association and is the author of Media Coverage of Crime and Criminal Justice.

Studies show that certain kinds of music tend to feature and even promote violence, especially in children and adolescents.

Rap Music Is Blamed for Promoting Violence

[Controversial musician] Marilyn Manson even got blamed for the Columbine High School shootings, even though the killers did not listen to his music.

Of course, rap music gets much of the blame. For example, the Prevention Research Center of the Pacific Institute for Research and Evaluation in Berkeley, Calif., suggests young people who listen to rap and hip-hop are more likely to abuse alcohol and commit violent acts.

And some claim increases in violence in their city are due to rap music!

Eric Armstrong analyzed lyrics from 490 rap songs produced by 13 different artists from 1987 to 1993. He found that 22% of gangsta rap music songs contain violent and misogynist lyrics. According to his study, the fastest selling rap album of all time—Eminem's *The Marshall Mathers LP*—contains 14 songs, and violent and misogynist lyrics are found in 11 (79%) of them: "Worse still, nine of the eleven songs depict killing women, with drowning becoming a new modus operandi. Comparing the lyric content of gangsta rap music's foundational period with that of Eminem shows the following: In terms of violent and misogynist lyrics, gangsta rap music (1987–1993) scores a 22 percent while Eminem (2000) reaches 78 percent."

Here are some examples of his music:

- "Kill You"

- "Criminal"

- "Role Model"

Does this matter?

Parents can help their teenagers by paying attention to their teenager's purchasing, downloading, listening and viewing patterns.

The American Academy of Child and Adolescent Psychiatry reports:

Singing and music have always played an important role in learning and the communication of culture. Children learn from what their role models do and say. For many years, some children's television very effectively used the combination of words, music and fast-paced animation to achieve learning.

Most parents are concerned about what their young children see and hear, but as children grow older, parents pay less attention to the music and videos that capture and hold their children's interest.

Some Teens Are at Greater Risk

Sharing music between generations in a family can be a pleasurable experience. Music also is often a major part of a teenager's separate world. It is quite common for teenagers to get pleasure from keeping adults out, which causes adults some distress.

A concern to many interested in the development and growth of teenagers is the negative and destructive themes of some kinds of music (rock, heavy metal, hip-hop, etc.), including best-selling albums promoted by major recording companies. The following themes, which are featured prominently in some lyrics, can be particularly troublesome:

- Drugs and alcohol abuse that is glamorized

- Suicide as an "alternative" or "solution"

- Graphic violence

- Sex which focuses on control, sadism, masochism, incest, children devaluing women, and violence toward women

Parents can help their teenagers by paying attention to their teenager's purchasing, downloading, listening and viewing patterns, and by helping them identify music that may be destructive. An open discussion without criticism may be helpful.

Music is not usually a danger for a teenager whose life is balanced and healthy. But if a teenager is persistently preoccupied with music that has seriously destructive themes, and there are changes in behavior such as isolation, depression, alcohol or other drug abuse, evaluation by a qualified mental health professional should be considered.

Music Videos Glorifying Violence Send the Wrong Message

Parents Television Council

The Parents Television Council is a nonpartisan educational organization advocating responsible entertainment for families and children.

The Parents Television Council joined with Industry Ears and the Enough Is Enough Campaign to condemn murder as depicted in Rihanna's latest music video, "Man Down," and call on Viacom to stop airing it. The video, which premiered on BET's [Black Entertainment Television] "106 & Park" on May 31 [2011], shows Rihanna in an implied rape scene with a man whom she later guns down in an act of premeditated murder.

Message of Retaliation Is Wrong

"'Man Down' is an inexcusable, shock-only, shoot-and-kill theme song. In my 30 years of viewing BET, I have never witnessed such a cold, calculated execution of murder in primetime. Viacom's standards and practices department has reached another new low," said Paul Porter, co-founder of Industry Ears and a former voice of BET.

"If Chris Brown [singer and former boyfriend who assaulted Rihanna] shot a woman in his new video and BET premiered it, the world would stop. Rihanna should not get a pass and BET should know better. The video is far from broadcast worthy," Porter stated.

"Parents Television Council Joins with Industry Ears, Enough Is Enough to Condemn Rihanna's 'Man Down' Video," parentstv.org, June 1, 2011. Copyright © 2011 by Parents Television Council. All rights reserved. Reproduced by permission.

"Rihanna's personal story and status as a celebrity superstar provided a golden opportunity for the singer to send an important message to female victims of rape and domestic violence. Instead of telling victims they should seek help, Rihanna released a music video that gives retaliation in the form of premeditated murder the imprimatur of acceptability. The message of the disturbing video could not be more off base," said Melissa Henson, director of communications and public education for the Parents Television Council.

"To make matters worse, Rihanna went to Twitter this week to tell her fans the video contains a 'very strong underlying message 4 girls like me.' A graphic portrayal of the singer getting back at an attacker by shooting him in cold blood in a crowded train station and then fleeing the scene is potentially the worst possible message that could be sent.

"No one questions that female pop stars can be profoundly influential in the lives of young girls. A new study in the *Journal of Children and Media* serves to further underscore that point, especially among girls ages nine to 11. We call on Viacom to immediately stop airing the video," Henson said.

"Once again BET has chosen the low road over the high road. Violence is a pervasive problem in all corners of our society and today's youth need more positive strategies for dealing with conflict than those portrayed in the Rihanna video. This video is one among several frequently played on Viacom music video networks that lyrically or graphically glorifies violence and other behavior inappropriate for teens and youth," said Pastor Delman Coates, founder of the Enough Is Enough Campaign.

"'Man Down' is a clear violation of BET's own programming guidelines shared with the public by Debra Lee, the chairman and CEO [chief executive officer] of BET Networks. I join with the Parents Television Council and Industry Ears in calling on Viacom executives to immediately pull the video from programs that are targeted to youth and teenagers," Coates concluded.

Listening to Rap Music Does Not Make Teens Violent

Jennifer Copley

A contributing writer for the website Suite101.com as well as other publications, Jennifer Copley is also a researcher and editor.

Studies have been conducted to assess the effects of listening to rap music on teenagers and young adults. Findings thus far are mixed, but overall they suggest that listening to rap music doesn't cause aggressive or deviant behaviour.

Does Rap Music Make Young People More Accepting of Crime and Violence?

Between 1979 and 1997, the percentage of rap songs with violent content increased steadily from 27% to 60%, and although rap songs often portrayed violence negatively in the past, a greater percentage of the more recent songs glamourize crime and aggression (Herd, 2009).

A study conducted by [J.] Johnson et al. (1995) found that young subjects who watched violent rap videos were more accepting of violent actions, particularly against women. Additionally, those who watched either violent or nonviolent rap videos were more inclined to express materialistic attitudes and favour acquiring possessions through crime, and they held more negative views on the likelihood of succeeding through academic pursuits. Another study conducted by the same group found that adolescent females, after watching a rap video depicting women in sexually subordinate roles, were more inclined to express acceptance of violence against women in a dating situation.

Overall, increased acceptance of crime and violence appears to be linked with viewing violent or sexist rap videos rather than listening to rap music on its own (Johnson et al., 1995). Also, [J.] Tanner et al. (2009) found that listening to rap is far more strongly correlated with property crimes than crimes of violence among urban youth, and the likelihood of committing such crimes is probably increased by poverty rather than musical preference.

Does Rap Music Promote Misogyny?

Young men who had little previous exposure to rap music were the subjects of an experiment in which researchers had one group listen to rap music with lyrics, another listen to rap music without lyrics, a third just read the lyrics, and a fourth group neither listen nor read. After the exposure, none of the subjects held more negative attitudes about women than they had before, but those who read or heard the lyrics were more inclined to express adversarial sexual beliefs (Wester et al., 1997).

Interestingly, another study found that university students who prefer heavy metal actually hold more hostile attitudes toward women, whereas their rap-loving peers tended to be more distrustful of the opposite sex (Rubin et al., 2001).

While a number of studies have associated lower grades with a preference for rap or heavy metal music, academic problems usually start before students develop a taste for these musical genres.

Overall, only rap music with misogynistic themes is likely to promote a greater acceptance of violence against women (Barongan & Hall, 1995), and many rap songs are not misogynistic or violent. [M.D.] Cobb and [W.A.] Boettcher III (2007) did find an increase in sexism among males who listened to non-misogynistic rap lyrics. However, the researchers assert that the music was simply activating pre-existing attitudes rather than causing subjects to become more sexist than they had been before the exposure.

Do Students Who Listen to Rap Music Engage in More Delinquent Behaviours?

Research has found that a preference for heavy metal or rap music is associated with higher rates of drug and alcohol use, arrests, and sexual promiscuity, but these problems often begin before young people start listening to rap or heavy metal. This indicates that the music doesn't cause behavioral problems or addiction; rather, it suggests that at-risk youth are more inclined to prefer heavy metal or rap music (Baker & Bor, 2008, Tatum, 1999).

[D.] Miranda and [M.] Claes (2004) found that rap fans were more likely to commit violent acts and use drugs, but there were differences based on subgenres of rap, with French rap and gangsta rap being associated with higher rates of deviancy and hip hop and soul linked to lower rates of problem behaviours.

Interestingly, Tanner et al's 2009 study found that delinquent activity among teenagers who prefered to listen only to rap music differed by race: White and Asian fans were more likely to commit both property crimes and violent crimes, whereas black rap lovers were no more likely to commit either violent or non-violent crimes than black fans of other musical genres.

Does Listening to Rap Music Have an Impact on Academic Achievement?

While a number of studies have associated lower grades with a preference for rap or heavy metal music, academic problems usually start before students develop a taste for these musical genres, so poor grades can't be blamed on the music. Interestingly, one study found that white students actually improved their academic performances after watching rap videos, as well as expressing more progressive attitudes (after watching politically focused rap videos, they were more inclined to support a liberal black political candidate)(Tatum, 1999). Unfortunately, there was no indication of similar research being conducted with black students.

Does Rap Music Affect Mood?

Listening to rap or heavy metal does not appear to increase suicidal ideation and anxiety, or adversely affect the self-esteem of college-aged men and women (Tatum, 1999).

> *There is no consistent evidence that rap music on its own ... significantly influences behaviors or attitudes.*

Oddly enough, a study conducted by Ballard & Coates (1995) found that students who listened to a nonviolent rap song experienced more depressive symptoms than those who listened to a violent rap song, but overall, rap songs were more inclined to generate angry emotions than heavy metal songs.

Has Rap Music Been Unfairly Maligned?

Some research suggests that people may have negative impressions of rap due to subconscious racism. Subjects who were given a violent lyrical passage were more inclined to rate it as dangerous or offensive if they believed it came from a rap song than if they were told that it originated from a country music song (Carrie, 1999).

It's also worth noting that in Marseille, France, rap and hip hop are thriving musical forms, and many residents believe that the positive effects of this music are the reason why poor North African neighborhoods in the region didn't suffer the rioting seen in other areas of Paris (Kimmelman, 2007).

Overall, there is no consistent evidence that rap music on its own (without videos) significantly influences behaviors or attitudes. Also, while those who are not fans of rap tend to assume that all songs in the genre focus on violent, criminal, or misogynistic themes, in reality, rap is a diverse genre, with many artists addressing important sociopolitical issues and positive themes.

References:

- Baker, F., & Bor, W. (2008). "Can Music Preference Indicate Mental Health Status in Young People?" *Australasian Psychiatry, 16*(4): 284–288.

- Ballard, M.E., & Coates, S. (1995). "The Immediate Effects of Homicidal, Suicidal, and Nonviolent Heavy Metal and Rap Songs on the Moods of College Students." *Youth and Society, 27*148–168.

- Barongan, C., & Hall, G.C.N. (1995). "The Influence of Misogynous Rap Music on Sexual Agression Against Women." *Psychology of Women Quarterly, 19*: 195–207.

- Carrie, F. (1999). "Who's Afraid of Rap: Differential Reaction to Music Lyrics." *Journal of Applied Social Psychology, 29*(4), 705–721.

- Cobb, M.D., & Boettcher, III, W.A. (2007). "Ambivalent Sexism and Misogynistic Rap Music: Does Exposure to Eminem Increase Sexism?" *Journal of Applied Social Psychology, 37*(12): 3,025–3,042.

- Herd, D. (2009). "Changing Images of Violence in Rap Music Lyrics: 1979–1997." *Journal of Public Health Policy, 30*(4): 395–406.

- Johnson, J.; Adams, M.; Ashburn, L.; & Reed, W. (1995). "Differential Gender Effects of Exposure of Rap Music on African American Adolescents' Acceptance of Teen Dating Violence." *Sex Roles, 33*(7/8): 597–605.

- Johnson, J.D.; Jackson, L.A.; & Gatto, L. (1995). "Violent Attitudes and Deferred Academic Aspirations: Deleterious Effects of Exposure to Rap Music." *Basic & Applied Social Psychology, 16*(1/2): 27–41.

- Kimmelman, M. (19 December 2007). "In Marseille, Rap Helps Keep the Peace." *New York Times, 157*(54163): E1–E5.

- Miranda, D., & Claes, M. (2004). "Rap Music Genres and Deviant Behaviours in French-Canadian Adolescents." *Journal of Youth and Adolescence, 33* 113–122.

- Rubin, A.M.; West, D.V.; & Mitchell, W.S. (2001). "Differences in Aggression, Attitudes Towards Women, and Distrust as Reflected in Popular Music Preferences." *Media Psychology, 3*: 25–42.

- Tanner, J.; Asbridge, M.; & Wortley, S. (2009). "Listening to Rap: Cultures of Crime, Cultures of Resistance." *Social Forces, 88*(2): 693–722.

- Tatum, B.L. (1999). "The Link Between Rap Music and Youth Crime and Violence: A Review of the Literature and Issues [HTML Version]." *Justice Professional, 11*(3).

- Wester, S.R; Crown, C.L.; Quatman, G.L.; & Heesacker, M. (1997). "The Influence of Sexually Violent Rap Music on Attitudes of Men with Little Prior Exposure." *Psychology of Women Quarterly, 21*(4): 497.

Violence in Music Videos Mirrors Violence in Society

Gil Kaufman

Gil Kaufman is a contributor to Rolling Stone, *among other publications.*

A day after the Parents Television Council [PTC] and other groups decried the violent murder scene in her new "Man Down" video, Rihanna took to the air and to Twitter to defend her clip from detractors.

"I'm a 23 year old rock star with NO KIDS! What's up with everybody wantin me to be a parent? I'm just a girl, I can only be your/our voice!" she wrote on Thursday [2011]. "Cuz we all know how difficult/embarrassing it is to communicate touchy subject matters to anyone especially our parents! And this is why! . . . Cuz we turn the other cheek! U can't hide your kids from society, or they'll never learn how to adapt! This is the REAL WORLD! . . . The music industry isn't exactly Parents R Us! We have the freedom to make art, LET US! It's your job to make sure they don't turn out like US."

Parents Television Council Condemns Rihanna Video

The PTC took issue with the opening scene in the video, in which Rihanna is shown shooting an unarmed man in the back of the head in the middle of a crowded train station. Viewers later learn that the act was in retaliation for a previous sexual assault.

The PTC, the Enough Is Enough campaign and the entertainment think tank Industry Ears released a statement on Wednesday condemning the video for what the group said was an apparent enticement to young women to turn to violence.

"'Man Down' is an inexcusable, shock-only, shoot-and-kill theme song," said Industry Ears co-founder Paul Porter.

The PTC lamented that Rihanna had a "golden opportunity" to use her celebrity status to send an important message to young girls and victims of rape and domestic violence with the clip, but had missed the mark. "Instead of telling victims they should seek help, Rihanna released a music video that gives retaliation in the form of premeditated murder the imprimatur of acceptability," said the PTC's Melissa Henson.

Rihanna Says Her Video Reflects the Real World

The singer later pleaded with her fans to stop making threats against members of the PTC, writing, "We love it, they don't . . . that is all, and the world keeps turning."

Though she has been a victim of domestic violence . . . Rihanna said she does not condone violence or murder.

She also called in to the BET [Black Entertainment Television] show "106 & Park" on Thursday night to defend the clip, saying she didn't set out to spark any controversy, but isn't surprised she did.

"Rape is, unfortunately, happening all over the world and in our own homes, and we continue to cover it up and pretend it doesn't happen," Rihanna said. "Boys and girls feel compelled to be embarrassed about it and hide it from everyone, including their teachers, their parents and their friends. That only continues to empower the abusers."

She noted that the song's lyrics clearly express the character's regret over her actions, and while the song doesn't mention rape, that was added to the video to make the story more complete. "Making that into a mini-movie or video, we needed to go back to why it happened," she explained. "Obviously, she's not a cold-blooded killer. It had to be something so offensive. And we decided to hone in on a very serious matter that people are afraid to address, especially if you've been victimized in this scenario."

Though she has been a victim of domestic violence—her ex, singer Chris Brown, pleaded guilty to felony assault against her in 2009—Rihanna said she does not condone violence or murder. "I've been abused in the past, and you don't see me running around killing people in my spare time," she said. "I just really want girls to be careful. Have fun, be sassy, be innocent, be sweet, be everything that you are. But just try not to be naive. That's not coming from a parent but from a peer."

CHAPTER 2

Is Exposure to Violence in Television and Movies Harmful?

Violent Youth: The Censoring and Public Reception of *The Wild One* and *The Blackboard Jungle*

Jerold Simmons

Jerold Simmons teaches American constitutional history at the University of Nebraska in Omaha. With Leonard J. Leff he coauthored the book The Dame in the Kimono.

At a time of transition for the Production Code Administration, Hollywood's self-regulatory censor body, a number of films pushed permissible boundaries regarding profanity and violence. Drawing on material from Production Code files, this paper discusses problems involved in the production and release of two films notorious for their depiction of violence and delinquency, *The Wild One* (Columbia, 1953) and *The Blackboard Jungle* (MGM, 1955).

Movie violence plagued Hollywood's censors. Since the notorious gangster cycle of the early 1930s, the staff of the Production Code Administration had sought to convince the film colony to cut back on the number of vicious killings and brutal fights in American pictures, but eliminating violence proved particularly troublesome. Some of the difficulty stemmed from the document the PCA was created to enforce: of the Code's twelve major sections, only two related in any fashion to violence, and even there the strictures were relatively general. The Code prohibited the depiction of 'wholesale slaughter', 'excessive brutality', the 'flaunting of weapons', and 'third degree methods'. 'Brutal killings' were 'not to be pre-

Jerold Simmons, "Violent Youth: The Censoring and Public Reception of 'The Wild One' and 'The Blackboard Jungle,'" *Film History*, Vol. 20, No. 3, July 2008. Copyright © 2008 by Indiana State University Press. All rights reserved. Reproduced by permission.

sented in detail', and the techniques used for murder were never to 'inspire imitation'. But the Code said nothing about beatings, blood and gore. More to the point, the manner in which the Code office operated limited its ability to control film violence.

The Code office staff, initially under long-time director Joseph Breen and after October 1954 under Geoffrey Shurlock, always preferred to remove objectionable material at the script level and was reluctant to order costly changes once filming had been completed. As Shurlock once observed, 'You ask for a cut in [a] finished picture and everybody blows their top'.[1] Because screenplays rarely provided a detailed description of how a fight, murder, or other brutal encounter would be filmed, the Code office was forced to rely on the director's discretion. If the staff suspected that a fight scene might become too violent, Breen or Shurlock would issue a warning, often reminding the director that it was 'unacceptable to show any kicking, kneeing, gouging or other forms of excessive brutality'.[2] But studios and directors knew that violence, like sex, enhanced screen excitement, so they often pressed the Code to its limits.

Occasionally, Breen cracked down by eliminating or modifying scenes showing explicit brutality or an excessive number of murders, but normally after a short period his interest waned and the violence returned. Shurlock, however, had less choice in the matter. Soon after he was elevated to director, two motion pictures, both aimed at the emerging youth market, focused the nation's attention on the issue of violence in American film. *The Wild One* (1954) and *The Blackboard Jungle* (1955) effectively illustrate the problems that scripts containing youthful violence posed for both Shurlock's staff and their opposite numbers at the British Board of Film Censors.

The British board operated much like Hollywood's Production Code Administration. Both originated as agencies created by the film industry in an effort to manage screen sex, violence and other offensive material that could lead to public regulation. Unlike the PCA, which operated under the authority of the American industry's trade association (The Motion Picture Association of America), the British board developed close ties with the government. Its director was normally a retired civil servant or government minister, and its staff maintained frequent contact with Whitehall. Nonetheless, the BBFC and the PCA employed similar procedures and standards. The British board applied many of the same restrictions concerning adultery, nudity, crime and violence enforced by the PCA, and as in Hollywood, most British producers found it advantageous to seek BBFC approval on story ideas and scripts well before filming began. There were, however, important differences. While the BBFC operated on precedent and used a set of written guidelines, the absence of a formal and binding code gave the British board greater flexibility than its American counterpart. More importantly, the board's classification system allowed its staff to place films containing adult material in specific categories that limited the admission of children. Their X rating, adopted in 1951, restricted the audience to those over 15, and the A rating permitted children only when accompanied by an adult. Together, these classifications enabled the BBFC to approve films aimed at mature tastes.[3]

The British board had long been critical of American screen violence. Like the Breen office, it had issued periodic warnings, deleted footage, and occasionally placed particularly violent films in its X classification. But in 1953 the BBFC cracked down with a vengeance. Over the next eighteen months it completely rejected seven American features and cut so much from two others that the distributors ordered them shelved. The resulting loss of an estimated two million dollars in British film rentals caught the industry's attention and forced Shurlock to look more closely at the problem of movie violence.[4] At roughly the same time, Tennessee's Senator Estes Kefauver announced his intention to resume an investigation into the causes of juvenile delinquency in America, promising to give special scrutiny to the charge that film violence conditioned the nation's youth toward antisocial conduct. Both the Kefauver Committee and the BBFC were particularly offended by *The Wild One* and *The Blackboard Jungle*.

Crime in the Streets: *The Wild One*

The Wild One taxed even Breen's relatively tolerant standards on violence. First submitted to the PCA in December 1952 as 'The Cyclists' Raid', the screenplay was based on a 1947 incident in which gangs of bikers invaded and brutalized Hollister, California. The title and several characters had been drawn from a Frank Rooney short story about the raid published in *Harper's*, but much of the dialogue came from interviews with active bikers. Director Laslo Benedek and screenwriter John Paxton spent several weeks researching the incident in Hollister, and producer Stanley Kramer personally interviewed a number of bikers. Kramer seems to have hoped at the outset to probe the motives and mindset of violent youth, or as Marlon Brando later put it, to explore 'why young people tend to bunch into groups that seek expression in violence'.[5] Yet the research yielded few clues as to motivation, and what started as social commentary quickly gave way to pure action. Paxton's script shocked the PCA readers in its unrestrained and unfocused violence. One staff member noted that it 'abounded' with 'fury, violence, lawlessness, the destruction of property, brutality, drunkenness, callousness and contempt for society'.[6] What worried Breen and his associates most was the impact 'The Cyclists' Raid' would have on younger viewers. 'The callousness of the young hoodlums in upsetting the normal tenor of life in a small town, the manner in which they panic the citizens, the ineffectiveness of law and order for the majority of the script, the brawling, drunkenness, vandalism and irresponsibility of the young men are, in our opinion, all very dangerous elements. They cannot help but suggest to younger members of the audience, it seems to us, the possibilities that lie in their power to get away with hoodlumism, if only they organize into bands'.[7]

It was [the] element of intimidation—this notion that a gang of young hoodlums could take control of a community and, for kicks, subject its citizens to threats and humiliation—that had first incurred the PCA's wrath.

Breen's letter rejecting the script prompted a lengthy meeting four days later in which Kramer, Benedek, and Paxton sought to convince Code officials Jack Vizzard and Milton Hodenfield of the merits of the project. Kramer used this opportunity to engage in some hastily devised damage control. He explained that Paxton's script had inadvertently omitted the central 'premise' of his film. That premise and the movie's central theme, he claimed, was supposed to be the redemption of Johnny, the leader of the Black Rebels. He would be rescued from a life of crime and anti-social behavior through the love of a good woman (Mary, the young waitress he came to care for). Kramer argued that for the plot to work, the cyclists had to engage in lawlessness and destructive behavior. The picture, in other words, had to be violent. But to pacify the Code officials, he promised to revamp the script in such a way as to eliminate at least sixty per cent of the 'hoodlumism'.[8] Kramer quit the meeting at lunchtime, but the other principals returned for a long afternoon session concentrating on the details. Benedek and Paxton promised to add a preface condemning the violence, to strengthen the character of the local sheriff, and to focus the script more tightly around the theme of rejuvenation. They continually pressed Vizzard and Hodenfield for some formal indication of script approval so they could proceed with the project, but the Code officers refused to act until they had seen the fully revised screenplay.

The following morning Vizzard received a call from Kramer's office asking again for formal script approval. Kramer had already spent $200,000 on the project and was committed to begin filming at the Columbia Ranch on 20 January 1953. With barely thirty days to prepare the sets, they needed to start work immediately. Vizzard refused to budge. Despite the concessions and promises of the previous day, he suggested that any action without an approved script would be 'highly speculative and very risky'.[9] Kramer called later to personally emphasize the urgency and to inform Vizzard that Paxton and Benedek were working hurriedly on a new scene-by-scene outline which he hoped would satisfy all remaining Code office concerns. Kramer assured Vizzard that the revisions would be complete by evening, and the two agreed on another conference the following day.

The new outline apparently impressed the censors. They always appreciated working with experienced producers who understood the requirements of the Code and tailored their product accordingly. In this case Kramer's 'obvious grasp of the Code difficulties' eased their fears and they granted the story tentative approval.[10] In an unusual concession, Breen's staff agreed to handle the revised script piece by piece, always a dangerous procedure in that action that might seem innocuous in an isolated scene might become far more ominous when set within the larger screenplay. But Kramer was an important producer, and with the shooting deadline fast approaching the concession seemed warranted. Over the next several weeks, Paxton forwarded sections of the script to the PCA and the staff responded with detailed suggestions. Nearly all focused on reducing the violence of the original. They warned against too much vigor in the rocking of the car by the youths in the street riot, against 'unnecessary brutality' in the fight scenes, and against 'kicking and gouging' throughout.[11] Kramer and Benedek complied with the instructions, and the feature moved swiftly through the Code machinery without further snags.

Released in December 1953, *The Wild One* showed the PCA's imprint. The textual preface, added to pacify Breen and his staff, warned the audience: 'This is a shocking story. It could never take place in most American towns—but it did in this one. It is a public challenge not to let it happen again.' Much of the violence and fury of Paxton's original script had been removed, and a strong voice condemning the biker's lawlessness had been added in the form of the county sheriff, who arrives near the end of the picture to restore order. While the young men received no formal punishment for their actions, the concluding scenes showing a reformed Johnny returning to Wrightsville alone were clearly designed to show the audience, and the PCA, that he had learned his lesson and had rejected his violent past. Yet *The Wild One* still contained much that could offend. While the violence had been muted, the element of gang intimidation remained. The Black Rebels and their rivals, the Beetles, take control of Wrightsville, conducting drag races in the streets, cowing the local police officer, and harassing the citizens. Near the film's climax they cut the community's phone lines and go on a drunken and destructive rampage through the streets. Curiously, *Variety's* reviewer found the actions of the citizens of Wrightsville even more unsettling than those of the bikers. In response to the gang rampage, merchants arm themselves and capture Johnny, subjecting him to a beating described by *Variety* as more 'vicious and vindictive' than anything perpetrated by the Black Rebels.[12]

It was this element of intimidation—this notion that a gang of young hoodlums could take control of a community and, for kicks, subject its citizens to threats and humiliation—that had first incurred the PCA's wrath. The fear that teenagers might find the bikers' conduct exciting and seek to emulate it had prompted Breen's initial rejection of the script. That element remained in the film. In contrast to the venal merchants, the cowardly cop, and the very square locals, Johnny and his gang attract the viewer and invite identification.

Yet after the hurried script negotiations of December 1952, the Code office readers never again raised this issue. Apparently, they were persuaded that Johnny's transformation from Black Rebel to solid citizen at the end of the film offered sufficient compensating moral values to offset the violence and intimidation.

Pictures like The Wild One . . . *generated mounting concerns about the portrait of America conveyed to foreign audiences.*

Many reviewers were not convinced. In spite of Johnny's redemption at the close, even liberal critics like Bosley Crowther of *The New York Times* found it difficult to get beyond the 'ugly, debauched and frightening view of a. . . menacing element of modern youth'. To Crowther, *The Wild One* was 'a picture of extraordinary candor and courage', but one that offered 'a glimpse of utter monstrosity' in the form of youthful rebellion.[13] Similarly, The *Hollywood Reporter's* Milton Luban praised Benedek's splendid craftsmanship but feared that the picture would appeal only to 'lawless juveniles who may well be inspired to go out and emulate the characters portrayed'.[14]

The reaction in Britain was even stronger. When the British Board of Film Censors first viewed the feature in January 1954, they found it 'dangerous in the extreme' and banned its release in the nation. Arthur Watkins, board secretary, provided the distributor with a summary of the objectionable elements:

The film deals with organized hooliganism and deliberate outrage of all law and order by a group of young toughs who at weekends ride about the countryside on motorcycles under an acknowledged leader. The story is said to be based on an actual incident in the United States which emphasizes the seriousness of all that happens, and the happenings include a long series of unprovoked insults and attacks on old and young alike in a small town, looting and destruction of property in a wild orgy, and finally the death of an innocent old man. The local police officer is helpless and ineffective and his daughter against her better nature 'falls for' the leader of the gang, demonstrating the morbid attraction which such young toughs can have for immature girls. When police reinforcements finally appear, the youths are allowed to get away with a mild and quite inadequate caution and so made to appear rather clever fellows than dangerous young fools.[15]

The concerns of the BBFC were heightened by the appearance of 'rowdy gangs of youths' in British cities. Dubbed 'teddy-boys' because of their Edwardian dress, these gangs engaged in the same kinds of violent brawls and lawless behavior that was attracting attention in America. Board members feared that *The Wild One* might 'aggravate this disturbing problem'. Since 'the hooliganism in the film [goes] unresisted and in the end virtually unpunished', it would likely attract the admiration of British youth 'rather than their censure'.[16] Board member John Trevelyan concluded that younger members of the audience would find only one message in *The Wild One*: 'If there were enough hoodlums and they behaved in a menacing way, they could get away with it'.[17])

Columbia went to extraordinary lengths over the next several years in an attempt to convince the British censors to lift their ban on *The Wild One*. Studio editors cut and recut the picture in an effort to remove the objectionable elements, but in the eyes of the British board, their alterations failed to change the film's central message. Efforts to bypass the board by appealing its ruling to the county councils that held final authority over local exhibition also failed. As a result, *The Wild One* was not approved for general release in Britain until 1967.[18]

Pictures like *The Wild One* also generated mounting concerns about the portrait of America conveyed to foreign audiences. With the emphasis of the Cold War shifting from direct Soviet-American confrontation toward the more subtle competition for support among non-aligned nations, State Department officials and others in government began to question the wisdom of exporting movies that featured the less wholesome elements of American society. Images of slums, poverty, greed, and racism did little to foster respect for America abroad. Teenage violence was even worse. Only days after Joe Breen's retirement in October 1954, the new Code Director, Geoffrey Shurlock, received a copy of a government report from Chile quoting at length from a story in the Communist newspaper, *El Siglo*. The paper ran a four-column spread which combined a commentary on *The Wild One* with an account of the brutal murder of two Brooklyn men by a gang of boys. The editorial concluded that: 'A savage society like the American capitalist society, where the only law is that of the jungle, produces a terrible deformation in the minds of the young. . . . Here we have in the flesh the "American way of life" that some wish to import to Chile'.[19] The report also included statements from anti-communist newspapers carrying the same theme. The most prominent of these was *El Debate*, whose editor found it 'astonishing that the United States allows a picture like *The Wild One* to be exported. . . . When he leaves the theater, the spectator asks himself, overwhelmed, 'Is this American civilization?'[20]

Leaders of the motion picture industry took such criticism seriously. With foreign rentals accounting for over forty per cent of annual revenue, the corporate directors in New York shuddered at any hint of pre-export censorship by the government. Beyond this, film industry leaders, like most Americans, were committed cold warriors. Their unabashed patriotism made them acutely sensitive to charges that American films might be serving as communist propaganda. Occasionally, these concerns led to friction between the corporate managers in New York and the filmmakers in Hollywood. When MGM executives in New York got wind that its California studio had purchased Evan Hunter's sensational novel *The Blackboard Jungle*, they feared another *Wild One*.

Crime in the Classroom: *The Blackboard Jungle*

Producer Pandro Berman remembered that East Coast management 'thought it an outrage that America was exposing our own weaknesses on the screen' and sought to block the project.[21] MGM production chief Dore Schary successfully battled the corporate barons for the right to make the picture, but vetoed location shooting in New York for fear that East Coast executives would get a copy of the script.[22] The rough-edged drama of one teacher's struggle to tame a violent high school gang was filmed in Los Angeles to avoid New York supervision.

The script that Berman submitted to the Production Code office in September 1954 had something for everyone: one teacher was sexually assaulted, two others were brutally beaten, knife fights and profanity abounded. Shurlock, just then in the process of taking over leadership of the agency, did his best to trim the worst. He warned that the 'tone of viciousness and brutality' that characterized the script had to be moderated, and suggested that the fights involving knives, tire chains, and other lethal weapons be removed or modified. The attempted rape of a teacher by a student could not be approved, nor could the 'sexual suggestiveness' in the teacher's conduct.[23] Richard Brooks, who adapted Hunter's novel for the screen and would direct the movie, agreed to trim some of the violence but insisted that the attempted rape was essential for the story's development. Shurlock eventually relented, but required that the assault be interrupted at the very beginning.

The script's profanity presented a special problem. Only days before the script's arrival, the Motion Picture Association Board of Directors had amended the Production Code so as to allow the use of the words 'damn' and 'hell' subject to the 'discretion and prudent advice of the Code Administration'.[24] Brooks sought to exploit the new loophole to the fullest by sprinkling the two words throughout the script. *The Blackboard Jungle* thus forced Shurlock to begin the process of defining when such words were and were not acceptable. His letter to MGM specified that 'hell' and 'damn' could be used only 'when they are absolutely necessary for proper plot motivation or characterization'. Shurlock determined that Brooks' script contained only one acceptable use of 'hell'. In the final classroom confrontation between the teacher, Richard Dadier (Glenn Ford) and the gang leader, Artie West (Vic Morrow), Dadier attempts to escort West to the principal's office. West pulls his switchblade and growls: 'You gonna make me, Daddy-o? How'd you like to go to hell!' In this single instance, the use of 'hell' was 'valid from a dramatic standpoint' and was 'therefore, acceptable'. All casual uses of the terms, as in 'Hey, what the hell', or 'the hell with you', were ordered out of the script. Perhaps in an effort to see how carefully the boys at the Code office were reading, Brooks also incorporated in the script the description of an exterior school wall containing a prominent 'F' followed by three letters that had been 'scrubbed away'. This, too, was to be eliminated as were 'dago', 'pope-lovers', and several other offensive phrases. Shurlock did allow the use of 'spic' and 'nigger', which were on the PCA's list of banned terms, in order to facilitate an important scene in which Dadier engages the class in a discussion of the dangers of name-calling. Despite the concessions, Brooks argued that Shurlock was being far too stringent, that the profanity was necessary to convey a sense of the students' rebelliousness.[25]

Shurlock eliminated most of the profanity, but *The Black-board Jungle* emerged from the Code office with much of the violence and intimidation intact. Crowther would later describe it as 'a blood-curdling, nightmarish picture of monsterous disorder in a public school', and Hedda Hopper called it the most brutal movie she had ever seen.[26] The delinquents that attend North Manual High School seem far more menacing than Brando's bikers. On the first day of class, as Dadier writes his name on the blackboard, a baseball whizzes past his head shattering pieces of slate. Shortly thereafter when he orders Artie West to remove his hat, West responds with an ominous threat: 'You ever try to fight 35 guys at once, teach?' At the end of the day, Dadier interrupts another student attempting to rape fellow first-year teacher Lois Hammond (Margaret Hayes) in the school library. The young man is scratched and bruised while attempting an escape by diving through a window, but the students believe Dadier inflicted the injuries. In retaliation Artie and six of his gang trap Dadier and the new math teacher, Josh Edwards (Richard Kiley), in an alley and savagely beat them. Back at school, in what becomes the film's signature scene, Artie's gang again mauls the idealistic Edwards, and for no apparent reason shatters his precious record collection. Edwards resigns but Dadier persists, and the classroom becomes a battleground in which he seeks to weaken West's hold over the students. To break Dadier's resolve, West launches a campaign of anonymous letters and phone calls to Dadier's wife (Anne Francis) alleging an affair between her husband and Miss Hammond.

Dadier's fellow teachers are no help in the struggle. Most of the veterans are either terrified of the hoodlums or cynical to the point of disinterest. They have accepted the school as a 'garbage can' in which delinquents are dumped and hold little hope of actually teaching them. Their function is to police the barbarians until they graduate or drop out. Dadier eventually wins the struggle, in part through innovative techniques (he shows a cartoon film of 'Jack and the Beanstalk' in order to engage the class in a discussion of ethics.), in part by winning over the moderate students, particularly Gregory Miller (Sidney Poitier). Yet his victory is not complete until the final violent confrontation in which he defies West's switchblade, disarms him, and, with the support of the class, marches him to the principal's office.

> *Shurlock was obviously committed to moving the Production Code away from the restrictive policies of the past and toward a more modern cinema that could depict contemporary problems in realistic ways.*

Shurlock must have known that a film portraying that much violence and intimidation in a public school would prompt serious criticism of both Hollywood and the Code office. Many were likely to see in *The Blackboard Jungle* the same dangers evident in *The Wild One*. Its portrait of student defiance and the intimidation of teachers was bound to provoke fears that teenagers would emulate the conduct of Artie and his gang. Brando and his bikers were obviously older, and while their conduct may have been frightening, it was beyond the experience of most of the nation's juveniles. Artie's gang, on the other hand, looked and acted like inner city teenagers. Their boredom, their frustration with class work that seemed irrelevant and with teachers who seemed not to care, gave them much in common with America's youth. If the prospect of emulation was frightening, so too was the portrait of the nation's schools that *The Blackboard Jungle* would carry abroad. Shurlock must have been conscious of the danger. The government report containing the editorials from Chile condemning *The Wild One* arrived at Shurlock's office in the midst of the Blackboard script negotiations. If *The Wild One* had prompted concerns about communist exploitation of American films, what would they say about *The Blackboard Jungle?*

Anticipating the fallout, Shurlock attempted to preempt the critics. At the beginning of November, in his first formal interview as the new Code office director, he warned the industry that its 'increasing tendency to go in for screen violence and brutality'[27] would lead to trouble. While not mentioning *The Blackboard Jungle*, he alluded to recent scripts he had read involving juveniles that contained 'an unusual . . . and overplayed accent on brutality'. Yet despite the warning, Shurlock showed little inclination to tame *The Blackboard Jungle*. When the Code office received the finished picture in February, he delegated the final review to staff members. They in turn required only very modest changes in the print, including the removal of a few seconds of film showing a chain wrapped around a student's hand, the ripping of Miss Hammond's blouse in the rape scene, and some minor cuts in the alley beating. Shurlock then issued the Code seal without further comment.[28]

Years later Shurlock explained to Murray Schumach why he had been so lenient with *The Blackboard Jungle*: 'If I tried to block the movie solely because it dealt with juvenile delinquency, I would be saying that movies must not deal with contemporary problems. And yet, juvenile delinquents act brutally and talk coarsely. So I ask that the brutality be toned down and the language be made less offensive. That was all I could ask for.'[29] The explanation may have been self-serving. Shurlock would ultimately receive more criticism for his approval of *The Blackboard Jungle* than for any other film he endorsed during his initial five years as Code director.[30] Yet the statement does reveal much about the new director's approach to his job. Shurlock was obviously committed to moving the Production Code away from the restrictive policies of the past and toward a more modern cinema that could depict contemporary problems in realistic ways. To do so he had to allow filmmakers much greater latitude as to subject matter and treatment. This he had done with Brooks and *The Blackboard Jungle*, but there would be a price.

Brooks and Berman hurried *The Blackboard Jungle* through production in just under ninety days. Much of the haste was prompted by their desire to exploit the new public visibility of juvenile delinquency. In October, the Senate subcommittee created to investigate juvenile crime reopened its hearings in Washington, and in January the subcommittee's executive director and chief counsel published the first of a series of five major articles on the topic in the Saturday Evening Post. Entitled 'The Shame of America', the stories drew attention to a dramatic increase in juvenile arrests and the mounting problem of teenage dropouts, drug use, and violent crime. The publicity was perfect for *The Blackboard Jungle*, and MGM took full advantage with ad copy like 'A Drama of Teenage Terror' and 'They Turned a School into a Jungle'. Initial television ads featured the rape scene, knife fight and other classroom confrontations.[31]

To further enhance the film's shock value, Brooks inserted Bill Haley's version of 'Rock Around the Clock' over the opening and closing credits. The linking of rock music and teenage rebellion created a potent marketing combination. The film propelled the song, which had been released in May 1954 with limited sales, to almost instant success. *The Blackboard Jungle* made 'Rock Around the Clock' an 'anthem of alienation' for teenage America and sent sales soaring.[32] It hit the Billboard singles chart in May 1955 and remained there for 29 weeks. The music, in turn, led *Variety* to predict that *The Blackboard Jungle* would be 'a controversial blockbuster' for MGM.[33]

As predicted, *The Blackboard Jungle* was a blockbuster. Because of the integrated classrooms and the positive role played by Poitier, MGM executives worried that the film would not be popular in the South. The picture's release came only ten months after the Supreme Court's decision in *Brown v. Board of Education*, a time of extreme tension and mounting violence over the issue of integration. But aside from minor problems with the local censors in Atlanta and Memphis, the picture did well in the South. Despite MGM's concerns, the film proved to be the studio's most successful release in nearly two years.[34] Theaters that rarely held a picture beyond one week ran *Blackboard* for three, and by May it was the top grossing movie in America. While critics divided over the movie's merits, teenagers found it compelling and attended again and again. Theater owners were sometimes less than thrilled with the results. With upwards of 75 per cent of the audience composed of rambunctious teens, owners worried about dancing in the aisles, teenage rumbles, and the loss of their older clients. A few cancelled the feature; one Boston owner cut the sound over the opening and closing credits so as to eliminate the stimulation provided by 'Rock Around the Clock'. But with Hollywood's traditional audience at home watching television, most owners considered any patron a good patron, irrespective of age, and *The Blackboard Jungle* came as a welcome addition to their marquees.[35]

Controversy followed the film wherever it showed. City officials or school administrators sought to have the feature blocked in Milwaukee, Minneapolis, Seattle, and Toronto, but in each case, the resulting publicity only seemed to enhance its appeal. The Memphis censor called it the 'vilest picture I've seen in 26 years' and banned it.[36] The mayor, seeking to avoid a court battle, quickly set aside the ban but limited attendance to adults. Teens responded by flocking to the theaters of West Memphis where the restriction did not apply. The Atlanta censor also banned the picture with similar results. Suburban theaters beyond the ban reaped the benefit until a federal district judge overruled the censor.[37] Teachers too, found much to criticize in *The Blackboard Jungle*. Many resented the portrayal of the teachers at North Manual as hardened cynics or brainless idealists. A few challenged the film's premise that successful teachers had to rely on tape recorders and motion pictures to reach their students, and still others complained that the filmmakers had exaggerated and sensationalized school violence. One administrator wrote the National Parent Teacher asking 'How can we ever recruit teachers when schools are shown as filled with young gangsters?'[38] The National Education Association convention in July included a special debate over the merits of *The Blackboard Jungle* in which Chicago's Superintendent of Schools condemned the film for making heroes of delinquents and for slandering both trade schools and their faculties.[39] MGM sought to counter the criticism by circulating positive teacher comments to newspapers and theater owners throughout the country. As protests mounted, however, more was needed. To appease local officials and teachers in New Brunswick, New Jersey, a regional distributor added a brief written statement at the end of the film praising the area's schools by name and inviting the viewers to visit and judge for themselves. MGM officials adopted the device and sent similar statements to distributors nationwide, but the protests continued.[40]

[The success of The Blackboard Jungle*] drove Hollywood toward the production of additional teenage dramas featuring more and more violence.*

Amid the controversy, Senator Kefauver announced that his subcommittee would hold a new set of public hearings that were to focus on the link between movie violence and juvenile delinquency. He specifically asked for the press books and other material related to the promotion of *The Blackboard Jungle*.[41] While Hollywood insiders predicted that the Senator was looking for an issue on which to build his campaign for the Democratic presidential nomination, they need not have worried. The public hearings did little to harm the industry.

Kefauver listened quietly while William Mooring, film editor of the *Catholic Tidings*, blasted Hollywood for its conscious promotion of violence. He cited eleven films as conclusive evidence, including both *The Wild One* and *The Blackboard Jungle*. But the remainder of the session was given over to fifteen industry spokesmen who both denied Mooring's contentions and promised to do better in the future. Dore Schary defended *Blackboard*'s violence as an essential ingredient in the film's larger purpose, which was to educate the public on both the dangers of delinquency and the need to improve the nation's schools. Shurlock also defended the industry. He noted the warning he had given the studios in October, but emphasized that the scripts he had read in recent months showed a marked retreat from the violence of late 1954. By the end of the two days of hearings, the Senator seemed convinced. His final comments included a mild warning for the industry, praise for Shurlock and his staff, and an expression of confidence that American motion pictures were getting better.[42]

Kefauver's comments may have brought relief in the film capital, but they did little to quiet the ongoing controversy over *The Blackboard Jungle*. Much as MGM's New York executives had feared, the picture reignited concerns that violent films could be 'hurting American prestige abroad'.[43] *Variety* featured a lengthy story citing industry sources who advocated the establishment of a voluntary system to identify and exclude such pictures from foreign distribution. Two weeks later, Senator Alexander Wiley, a member of the powerful Foreign Relations Committee, expanded on this theme in a Loyalty Day address in Wisconsin. Wiley condemned the export of movies that 'portrayed an America of sex, sin and sadism, of gangsterism, corruption, filth and degradation'.[44] The federal government was spending $80 million a year to promote a positive image abroad, he continued, only to see the entire effort undermined by a few ugly motion pictures. Wiley's speech suggested an ominous trial balloon and intensified Hollywood concerns that the government might seek to establish some sort of export censorship board. The controversy persisted over the summer, culminating at the end of August when America's Ambassador to Italy, Clare Boothe Luce, threatened to leave the Venice Film Festival if *The Blackboard Jungle* was shown there. Ambassador Luce felt the picture 'would create a seriously distorted impression of American youth and American public schools and, thus, abet the anti-U.S. propaganda of the Communists in Italy'.[45] Festival authorities quickly cancelled the exhibition, but the press coverage surrounding the incident made *Blackboard* 'one of the most highly publicized films in the worldwide market'.[46]

Luce's action worked perfectly for MGM. The picture was still in second run theaters in the United States and Canada, and was just being released throughout Europe. *Variety* estimated the furor created by Luce could mean as much as an additional one million dollars in box office receipts. Over the next several months, *Blackboard* out-performed all other American films in Europe and dominated markets ranging from Australia to Egypt.[47]

As always in the film business, controversy paid dividends. *The Blackboard Jungle* went on to become MGM's most successful release of 1955. Produced on a budget of $900,000, it generated well over $9 million in receipts.[48] Its success, combined with that of *Rebel Without a Cause* (released in October of 1955), drove Hollywood toward the production of additional teenage dramas featuring more and more violence. None, however, would generate the controversy and few would produce the profits of *The Wild One* and *The Blackboard Jungle*.

Notes

1. James M. Wall, unpublished Oral History with Geoffrey Shurlock, Louis B. Mayer/American Film Institute Film His-

tory Program, July 1970, 263. A copy of this interview is in the American Film Institute Library in Los Angeles.

2. Breen to Victor Saville of Parklane Pictures, 10 April 1953, I, the Jury file, Production Code Administration (PCA) Collection, Margaret Herrick Library, Academy of Motion Picture Arts and Sciences, Beverly Hills, California.
3. On the origin and operations of the British Board of Film Censors, see James C. Robertson, The Hidden Cinema: British Film Censorship in Action, 1913–1972 (London: Routledge, 1989).
4. Fay Allport, European Manager of the Motion Picture Association of America, to Geoffrey M. Shurlock, Director of the Production Code Administration, n.d. (probably May 1955), Box 711/22417, Universal Studios Collection, Special Collections, Doheny Library, University of Southern California.
5. Gary Carey, Marlon Brando: The Only Contender (New York: St. Martin's, 1972), 90–91.
6. Jack Vizzard file memo, 17 December 1952, The Wild One PCA file,
7. Breen to George Glass of Stanley Kramer Productions, 12 December 1952, The Wild One PCA file.
8. Vizzard file memo, 17 December 1952, The Wild One PCA file.
9. Ibid.
10. Breen to Stanley Kramer Productions, 18 December 1952, The Wild One PCA file.
11. Breen to George Glass, a Kramer associate, 7 January 1953 and 18 February 1953, The Wild One PCA file.
12. Variety (23 December 1953): 15.
13. New York Times (31 December 1953): 9.
14. The Hollywood Reporter (23 December 1953), The Wild One PCA clippings file. The Catholic Legion of Decency rated The Wild One 'B' ('morally objectionable') because of its 'excessive brutality'.

15. Arthur Watkins to Fay Allport, 22 March 1955, Box 711/ 22417, Universal Studios Collection, Special Collections, Doheny Library, University of Southern California.

16. Ibid.

17. John Trevetyan, What the Censor Saw (London: Michael Joseph, 1973), 152.

18. On the BBFC's long struggle with Columbia over The Wild One, see Robertson, The Hidden Cinema, 104–110. The film was also banned by the provincial censors in Alberta and Quebec and was released in British Columbia only after approval by an appeals board. The state censors in Massachusetts, Kansas, Pennsylvania, and Ohio, however, approved the picture without eliminations or comment.

19. Walton B. Thomas to Shurlock, 26 October 1954, The Wild One PCA file.

20. Ibid.

21. Quoted in the Los Angeles Herald Examiner (13 January 1983), The BlackBoard Jungle PCA clippings file.

22. Ibid.

23. Shurlock to Dore Schary, 20 September 1954, The Blackboard Jungle PCA file.

24. Variety (15 September 1954): 3. On the Code and profanity, see Jerold Simmons, "A Damned Nuisance: The Production Code and the Profanity Amendment of 1954," Journal of Popular Film and Television 25 (1997): 76–82.

25. Shurlock to Schary, 20 September and 22 October 1954, The Blackboard Jungle PCA file.

26. New York Times (21 March 1955): 21. Hopper is quoted in Mark Thomas McGee and R.J. Robertson, The J.D. Films: Juvenile Delinquency in the Movies (Jefferson, N.C.: McFarland & Company, 1982), 29.

27. Variety (3 November 1954): 3.

28. E. Dougherty file memo, 7 February 1955, The Blackboard Jungle PCA file.

29. Murray Schumach, The Face on the Cutting Room Floor: The Story of Movie and Television Censorship (New York: Da Capo, 1964), 176.

30. This observation is Shurlock's from a presentation that he made to Richard MacCann's film class on 11 May 1959. A tape of the presentation is in Special Collections, Doheny Library, University of Southern California.

31. McGee and Robertson, 27. Network censors forced the removal of the rape scene. Variety (23 March 1955): 10.

32. R. Serge Denisoff and William D, Romanowski, Risky Business: Rock in Film (New Brunswick: Transaction Publishers, 1991), 12.

33. Variety (2 March 1955): 16.

34. Variety (8 February 1956): 5.

35. Variety (18 May 1955): 5, (8 June 1955): 7.

36. Box Office (2 April 1955), The Blackboard Jungle PCA clippings file.

37. Variety (8 June 1955): 5; (29 June 1955): 20; (13 July 1955): 7.

38. Quoted in William D. Boutwell, "What's Happening in Education?" National Parent Teacher 49 (May 1955): 15.

39. Variety (13 July 1955): 15.

40. Variety (20 April 1955): 7.

41. Kefauver asked for materials related to only one other film, Son of Sinbad, a Howard Hughes production. Variety (25 May 1955): 24. Members of Kefauver's staff visited the PCA's office and read the correspondence on The Blackboard Jungle and other films containing violence. Wall, Oral History with Geoffrey Shurlock, 165.

42. U.S. Senate, Hearings Before the Subcommittee to Investigate Juvenile Delinquency, Motion Pictures, 15–18 June 1955.

43. Variety (20 April 1955): 7.

44. Quoted in Variety (4 May 1955): 3.

45. Quoted in Robinson McllvaineIncident," "Department Reply to Protest on Blackboard Jungle Incident," U.S. Department of State Bulletin 33 (1955): 537.

46. Variety (14 September 1955): 5.

47. Foreign censors often trimmed the more violent scenes in The Blackboard Jungle before local release, but only Italy, perhaps in deference to Ambassador Luce, banned the picture. Variety (25 April 1956): 5. The British Board of Film Censors at first refused it a certificate but eventually relented. The BBFC insisted on twenty cuts involving over six minutes of running time. An itemized list of the cuts is provided in Robertson, 116.

48. Los Angeles Herald Examiner (13 January 1983), The Blackboard Jungle PCA clippings file.

Violence on Television Can Contribute to Aggressive Behavior

Kyla Boyse

Kyla Boyse is a registered nurse who consults for the University of Michigan Health System.

Television (TV) has its good side. It can be entertaining and educational, and can open up new worlds for kids, giving them a chance to travel the globe, learn about different cultures, and gain exposure to ideas they may never encounter in their own community. Shows with a prosocial message can have a positive effect on kids' behavior; programs with positive role models can influence viewers to make positive lifestyle changes. However, the reverse can also be true: Kids are likely to learn things from TV that parents don't want them to learn. TV can affect kids' health, behavior and family life in negative ways.

Television Has Positive and Negative Aspects

It's worthwhile for parents to think about what role they want TV to play in their family. Consider:

- A great deal is known about children and television, because there have been thousands of studies on the subject. Researchers have studied how TV affects kids' sleep, weight, grades, behavior, and more. It's worth looking at what the research says when deciding how to manage television in your family.

- Spending time watching TV can take time away from healthy activities like active play outside with friends, eating dinner together as a family, or reading. TV time also takes away from participating in sports, music, art or other activities that require practice to become skillful.

- TV viewing starts earlier than other forms of media—often beginning before age two. In recent years, TV, video and DVD programs geared to babies and toddlers have come on the market—and now even a cable channel for babies. We don't know yet what effect TV-viewing by babies may have on their development. We do know that time spent watching TV replaces time spent interacting with caregivers and other children. Social interaction is critical to a baby's healthy development.

Repeated exposure to TV violence makes children less sensitive toward its effects on victims.

How Big a Presence Is TV in Kids' Lives?

- TV viewing among kids is at an eight-year high. On average, children ages 2–5 spend 32 hours a week in front of a TV—watching television, DVDs, DVR and videos, and using a game console. Kids ages 6–11 spend about 28 hours a week in front of the TV. The vast majority of this viewing (97%) is of live TV.

- 71% of 8- to 18-year-olds have a TV in their bedroom; 54% have a DVD/VCR player, 37% have cable/satellite TV, and 20% have premium channels.

- Media technology now offers more ways to access TV content, such as on the Internet, cell phones and iPods. This has led to an increase in time spent viewing TV, even as TV-set viewing has declined. 41% of TV-viewing is now online, time-shifted, DVD or mobile.

- In about two-thirds of households, the TV is "usually" on during meals.

- In 53% of households of 7th- to 12th-graders, there are no rules about TV watching.

- In 51% of households, the TV is on "most" of the time.

- Kids with a TV in their bedroom spend an average of almost 1.5 hours more per day watching TV than kids without a TV in the bedroom.

- Many parents encourage their toddlers to watch television. . . .

What About TV and Aggressive or Violent Behavior?

Literally thousands of studies since the 1950s have asked whether there is a link between exposure to media violence and violent behavior. All but 18 have answered, "Yes." The evidence from the research is overwhelming. According to the AAP [American Academy of Pediatrics], "Extensive research evidence indicates that media violence can contribute to aggressive behavior, desensitization to violence, nightmares, and fear of being harmed." Watching violent shows is also linked with having less empathy toward others.

- An average American child will see 200,000 violent acts and 16,000 murders on TV by age 18.

- Two-thirds of all programming contains violence.

- Programs designed for children more often contain violence than adult TV.

- Most violent acts go unpunished on TV and are often accompanied by humor. The consequences of human suffering and loss are rarely depicted.

- Many shows glamorize violence. TV often promotes violent acts as a fun and effective way to get what you want, without consequences.

- Even in G-rated, animated movies and DVDs, violence is common—often as a way for the good characters to solve their problems. Every single U.S. animated feature film produced between 1937 and 1999 contained violence, and the amount of violence with intent to injure has increased over the years.

- Even "good guys" beating up "bad guys" gives a message that violence is normal and okay. Many children will try to be like their "good guy" heroes in their play.

- Children imitate the violence they see on TV. Children under age eight cannot tell the difference between reality and fantasy, making them more vulnerable to learning from and adopting as reality the violence they see on TV.

- Repeated exposure to TV violence makes children less sensitive toward its effects on victims and the human suffering it causes.

- A University of Michigan researcher demonstrated that watching violent media can affect willingness to help others in need.

- Viewing TV violence reduces inhibitions and leads to more aggressive behavior.

- Watching television violence can have long-term effects:

- A 15-year-long study by University of Michigan researchers found that the link between childhood TV-violence viewing and aggressive and violent behavior persists into adulthood.

- A 17-year-long study found that teenaged boys who grew up watching more TV each day are more likely to commit acts of violence than those who watched less.

- Even having the TV on in the home is linked to more aggressive behavior in 3-year-olds. This was regardless of the type of programming and regardless of whether the child was actually watching the TV....

Can TV Scare or Traumatize Kids?

Children can come to view the world as a mean and scary place when they take violence and other disturbing themes on TV to be accurate in real life.

- Symptoms of being frightened or upset by TV stories can include bad dreams, anxious feelings, being afraid of being alone, withdrawing from friends, and missing school.

- Fears caused by TV can cause sleep problems in children.

- Scary-looking things like grotesque monsters especially frighten children aged two to seven. Telling them that the images aren't real does not help because kids under age eight can't always tell the difference between fantasy and reality.

- Many children exposed to scary movies regret that they watched because of the intensity of their fright reactions.

- Children ages 8–12 years who view violence are often frightened that they may be a victim of violence or a natural disaster.

- Violent threats shown on TV can cause school-aged kids (8–12) to feel fright and worry. When the threat is shown as news it creates stronger fears than when it is shown as fictional.

The Combination of Humor and Violence in Television Advertising Is Increasing

Benjamin J. Blackford et al.

Benjamin J. Blackford is an assistant professor of marketing and management at Northwest Missouri State University.

A bowling ball falls on a man's head to advertise a soft drink. Employees hurl a coworker out a window because of the mere suggestion that a specific beer should no longer be provided at meetings in order to reduce expenses. In another office setting, coworkers use a snow globe to break into a snack machine in pursuit of a certain snack food and to injure a supervisor. This is but a snapshot of the television commercials being aired that use humor in combination with violent acts to promote various products. How common is media content such as this in commercials? What effect does it have on the audience's reaction to the ad?

Studies on the Combination of Humor and Violence

The effects of viewing violent media are the subject of a large body of research across a number of disciplines including psychology, sociology, public policy, law, and marketing. Initial research in this area began to appear in the mid-1950s with a variety of studies. For example, [Albert] Bandura, [Dorothea] Ross, and [Sheila A.] Ross found that children who viewed live violent acts or televised violent acts tended to imitate these actions and engage in more violent actions themselves.

A recent [2008] review article by [John P.] Murray identified 1,945 research articles in the last 50 years examining the effects of television. Of these articles, approximately 600 focused on the issue of violence.

A related topic that has received limited attention in the literature is the use of humor in combination with the portrayal of violence. Such studies have generally found that the use of humor in conjunction with violence lessens the perception of violence. [Cynthia M.] King suggests one reason for using humor in combination with violence is to relieve or reduce audience stress from dramatic scenes. Humor may also serve to suggest to the audience that the events are not to be taken seriously. If the audience is affected by this cue, humor may trivialize the violence that is occurring, as suggested by [W. James] Potter and [Ron] Warren. Potter and Warren raise a concern, based on work by Bandura, that the trivialization of violence leads to a greater likelihood of such acts being imitated. In fact, Potter and Warren use the term "camouflage" to refer to the consumer's reaction to violence in the presence of humor, whereas [Erica] Scharrer et al. use the term "desensitize." If this is the case, it becomes important to identify how often humor is combined with violence in various forms of media, as this combination may have an influence as large as or larger than the display of violent acts in isolation.

Trivialized violence is the most likely to be imitated.

Given the potential adverse consequences attributable to combining these factors, this research seeks to provide further insight into the prevalence of the use of humor in combination with violence and their joint influence on ad popularity. Prior content analyses have approached this issue in a variety of ways, including analysis of violence in commercials during sporting events, as well as examinations of combinations of violence and humor occurring during nightly television programming and prime-time television commercials. Our study combines the approach of several of those just mentioned, as we examine violence and humor as depicted in television commercials occurring during a sporting event for three non-consecutive years over a period of five years.

Our research also investigates the likability of these commercials by integrating results from two ratings systems of commercial popularity. As such, three primary research questions were identified for this study: (1) How often are violence and humor combined in commercials aired during the Super Bowl? (2) How has this changed since 2005? and (3) Is there an association between the combination of humor and violence and the likability of ads? . . .

The Humor and Violence Interface

As noted earlier, there is only limited literature investigating the role of the desensitization of violence through the use of humorous contexts. Potter and Warren investigated the humor/violence interface in the context of television programming and found that comedy programs contained more violent acts per hour than other programming. More specifically, they observed 5,970 violent acts during 168 hours of programming, with 31% of these acts involving humorous content. Based on their results, Potter and Warren state that humor is not being used to reduce aggression in viewers by providing a break from violent content, but rather to trivialize the violence. This is of special concern because trivialized violence is the most likely to be imitated. Research has also found humor to have a significant negative correlation with the perceived violence in a program. Similarly, Bandura found that perpetrators of violent acts in television programs use humor to dehumanize victims to undermine the emotional responses from viewers.

Scharrer et al. specifically considered combinations of humor and violence in advertising. Their sample included 536 commercials containing aggressive behavior during a week of prime-time programming on six major broadcast networks. These commercials represented 12.3% of the total commercials during that time. Once again, advertisements for movie and television programs were the most likely to contain violent actions. Over half (53.5%) of the commercials included humorous elements. If the movie and television program ads were not considered, 87.7% of the violent commercials included humor.

We expand on this prior work in a number of ways. First, we analyze longitudinally [over a period of time] the occurrence of humor and violence in advertising in a different media context (during a highly watched sporting event, i.e., the Super Bowl) and through the inclusion of a richer set of humor and violence variables. In addition, in our study, we do not analyze duplicate commercials, as was the case in Scharrer et al., which we believe provides a more conservative assessment of the incidence of commercials that combined humor and violence. Also, we incorporated consumer judges to identify the humorous/violent acts in the commercials, rather than the researchers themselves or graduate assistants as in prior research. This provides insight into how the "average" consumer views violence and humor in advertisements. Finally, we also include currently available assessments of commercial popularity to gauge consumer opinion of commercials that combine acts of humor and violence. While prior research has addressed some of these areas, there has been no study to our knowledge that has taken all the above approaches into account. Further, we investigate the relationship between humor, violence, and their combination in terms of ad popularity, which has not been done heretofore. . . .

As was mentioned previously, the combination of humor and violence has the potential to desensitize viewers to violent acts and add to the likability of advertisements. Thus, this research was guided by three primary research questions that guide our understanding of the frequency and likability of the phenomenon and how it has changed over time. The discussion of the results addresses each research question in the order in which they were presented in the study.

How Often Are Violence and Humor Combined in Commercials Aired During the Super Bowl?

Several interesting findings, emerge from the results addressing the first research question. [These results come from a study of the 2005 Super Bowl advertisements]. The content analysis identified 234 total acts of violence (humorous and nonhumorous) in the approximately one hour and 50 minutes of commercials, a rate of 2.13 violent acts per minute. Out of all the commercials, 86, or 47.8%, were identified by at least one rater as containing a violent act. Of the 234 violent acts, 89 occurred outside of a humorous context. Only seven of the commercials containing violence were completely lacking in humor. There were 377 humorous incidents that did not include violence. Out of 180 commercials, 86 contained humor with no reference to violence by any rater. A total of 9 commercials (5%) contained no acts of violence, humor, or the combination coded by any of the raters.

Humor and violence were combined in 143 acts, representing 61.3% of all violent acts. In addition, 27.5% of all humorous acts were tied to a violent act. Just under 40% of all commercials aired were identified by at least one rater as containing an act combining violence and humor. Eight additional commercials contained acts of both violence and humor, but no acts that combined both. It comes as no surprise that 71 of these acts combining humor and violence were in conjunction with the "aggressive" dimension of humor, more than twice the number of acts for the next category, self-defeating.

How Has This Changed Since 2005?

The second research question concerned how humor and violence in Super Bowl commercials has changed since 2005. . . . It is interesting to note that instances of humor, violence, and the combination thereof all increased year to year, with the greatest increase occurring between 2007 and 2009. The 2009 Super Bowl commercials contained on average almost three times as many violent acts and acts combining humor and violence when compared to 2005, which represents a substantial increase given that it occurred over a time span of only five years. There was also an increase of almost 50% between 2005 and 2009 in the number of humorous acts identified.

Is There an Association Between the Combination of Humor and Violence and the Likability of the Ads?

The final research question asked how humor and violence influence the audience. To answer this question, two different independent rankings (the *USA Today* AdMeter and the AdBowl.com ballot) of consumers' reactions to Super Bowl commercials in terms of popularity were obtained for the three years sampled. . . .

This combination of humor and violence desensitizes viewers in terms of reacting negatively to the violence.

Results indicated a positive relationship between the combination of violence/humor acts and commercial popularity. . . .

Overall, our findings suggest that the most popular commercials during a Super Bowl will be those that include acts combining humor and violence. . . . We also note an upward trend in these acts over the years included in this study. Acts of violence and acts combining humor and violence have both increased greatly, in both cases more than doubling when 2005 and 2009 are compared.

Implications

That the number of acts including violence and violence and humor in Super Bowl commercials has increased by approximately 133% and 135%, respectively, over the five-year time span should be of concern to members of the academic community. Furthermore, we find that the portrayal of violence is unrealistic for several reasons. Some violent acts (10%) are shown to reward the perpetrator for their actions. The vast majority also depict no harm to the victim (90%) and no punishment for the perpetrator (98%). Perhaps even more troubling is that at least some of these violent but humorous commercials were well liked by viewers. Our analyses indicated that positively rated ads had significantly more acts that combined violence and humor than did those rated in the bottom 10 by consumers. Clearly, the combination of humor and violence seems to appeal to consumers. Research is needed to investigate the effects of viewers (especially children) seeing such acts in a positive context.

We agree with previous researchers who assert that this combination of humor and violence desensitizes viewers in terms of reacting negatively to the violence, thus subtly resulting in the conclusion that violence is acceptable if presented in a humorous context. The desensitization to violent portrayals that may arise when violence is combined with humor appears to be an appealing mix to some viewers, at least based on our popularity analyses. . . .

Perhaps most significant is that our Ad Meter and AdBowl information indicates viewers find these commercials more than merely acceptable; they also like at least some of them.

Thus, combining humor with violence appears to not only lessen the impact of violent portrayals but, more important, may also result in increased liking of violent depictions when they are shown in a humorous context. This would indeed be an unfortunate outcome of these commercial formats if viewers actually find violence more acceptable and likable when portrayed with humorous overtones. . . .

Exposure to Media Violence Increases Aggressive and Violent Behavior

Craig A. Anderson and Soledad Liliana Escobar-Chaves

Craig A. Anderson is a professor of psychology at Iowa State University and Soledad Liliana Escobar-Chaves is an assistant professor of health promotion and behavioral sciences at the University of Texas School of Public Health.

The extent to which media violence causes youth aggression and violence has been hotly debated for more than fifty years. Despite many reports that exposure to violent media is a causal risk factor, the U.S. public remains largely unaware of these risks, and youth exposure to violent media remains extremely high. Among the public advisories that have been generally ignored are congressional hearings in 1954, U.S. surgeon general reports in 1972 and 2001, a National Institute of Mental Health report in 1982, and a Federal Trade Commission report in 2000. In addition to government studies, reports have been issued by scientific organizations such as the American Psychological Association (in 1994, 2000, and 2005), the American Academy of Pediatrics, the American Academy of Child and Adolescent Psychiatry, the American Medical Association, the American Academy of Family Physicians, and the American Psychiatric Association.

The most recent [2003] thorough review of the research on media violence, by an expert panel convened by the U.S. surgeon general, concluded, "Research on violent television and films, video games, and music reveals unequivocal evidence that media violence increases the likelihood of aggressive and violent behavior in both immediate and long-term contexts." Hundreds of original empirical studies of the link between media violence and aggression have been conducted, and numerous reviews of those studies—both narrative and statistical—have come to the same conclusion. Indeed, one analysis found clear evidence that exposure to media violence increases aggressive behavior as early as 1975.

The newest form of media violence—violent video games played on computers, video game consoles, handheld systems, the Internet, and even cell phones—also is the fastest growing. Although most youth still spend more time each week watching TV, including movies, than playing video games, the time they spend with video games is increasing rapidly, and a growing share of youth is spending many hours playing video games. For example, about 90 percent of U.S. youth aged eight to eighteen play video games, with boys averaging about nineteen hours a week. Annual surveys of college freshmen over time reveal that as twelfth graders they spend ever-increasing amounts of time playing video games. The finding is especially true for boys. . . .

We review evidence on the link between youth violence and violence on television and film and on video games. We could find no studies on the effects of violence in advertising on aggressive or violent behavior, but the effects of such violent content are likely to be similar.

Television and Movie Violence and Violent Behavior

Television and movie violence are the most extensively researched forms of media violence. Studies using all three major research designs have all reached the same conclusion—exposure to television and movie violence increases aggression and violence.

Experimental studies [studies in which the researcher controls all the risk factors] have shown that even a single exposure increases aggression in the immediate situation. For example, Kaj Bjorkqvist randomly assigned one group of five- to six-year-old Finnish children to watch violent movies, another to watch nonviolent ones. Raters who did not know which type of movie the children had seen then observed them playing together in a room. Children who had just watched the violent movie were rated much higher on physical assault and other types of aggression. Other experiments have shown that exposure to media violence can increase aggressive thinking, aggressive emotions, and tolerance for aggression, all known risk factors for later aggressive and violent behavior.

The most popular video games played by youth contain violence. Even children's games ... are likely to contain violence.

Many cross-sectional studies [studies that look at a group at one point in time] have examined whether people who view many violent TV shows and movies also tend to behave more aggressively. Such studies generally find significant positive correlations. For example, one group of researchers studied the links between "aggressive behavioral delinquency," such as fighting and hitting, and TV violence viewing in samples of Wisconsin and Maryland high school and junior high school students. They found significant positive links between TV violence exposure and aggression for both boys and girls. Another research team reported 49 percent more violent acts in the past six months by heavy viewers of TV violence than by light viewers.

Researchers also have used longitudinal studies [studies over a period of time] to investigate television violence effects, using time periods that range from less than one year to fifteen years. One research team studied a group of six- to ten-year-olds over fifteen years. They found that both boys and girls who viewed television violence committed more aggression (physical, verbal, and indirect) during young adulthood. The study found the same link when the outcome examined was outright physical violence, such as punching, beating, choking, threatening, or attacking with a knife or gun. This media violence study is one of the few to include measures of violent crime. Because it is a well-conducted longitudinal study, it lends considerable strength to the view of media violence as a causal risk factor for aggression, violence, and violent crime. Interestingly, although frequent exposure to TV violence during childhood was linked to high levels of adulthood aggression, high aggressiveness during childhood did not lead to frequent viewing of television violence in adulthood.

Violent Video Games and Violent Behavior

The most popular video games played by youth contain violence. Even children's games (as designated by the industry-sponsored Entertainment Software Ratings Board) are likely to contain violence. More than 30 percent of games rated "E" (suitable for everyone) contain a violence descriptor; more than 90 percent of "E10+" games (suitable for those ten years and older) contain a violence descriptor. About 70 percent of fourth to twelfth graders report playing "Mature"-rated games (suitable for those seventeen and older), which contain the most graphic violence of all.

Research on video game violence is less extensive than that on TV and film violence, but the findings are essentially the same. Experimental studies in field and laboratory settings generally find that brief exposure to violent video games increases aggressive thoughts, feelings, and behavior. For example, one laboratory study assigned children and college students randomly to play either a children's video game that involved shooting cartoon-like characters or a nonviolent children's video game. Later, all participants completed a standard laboratory task that measures physical aggression. Those who had played the violent children's game displayed a 40 percent higher aggression rate than those who had played a nonviolent game. The effect was the same for both elementary school children and college students. In a field experiment, children were randomly assigned to play either a violent or nonviolent video game and then were observed by trained coders during a free-play period. The children who had played the violent game displayed significantly more physical aggression than those who had played a nonviolent game.

Media violence exposure has a larger effect on later violent behavior than does substance abuse, abusive parents, poverty, living in a broken home, or having a low IQ.

To date, the only published longitudinal study that clearly delineates the possible influence of violent video games used a relatively short time span of six months. The researchers conducting the study assessed the media habits and aggressive tendencies of elementary school children, as well as a host of control variables, twice within a school year. The children who were heavily exposed to video game violence early in the school year became relatively more physically aggressive by the end of the year, as measured by peers, teachers, and self-reports. Cross-sectional studies have also found positive correlations between exposure to violent video games and various forms of aggression, including violent behavior and violent crimes.

All three types of studies have also linked violent video games to a host of additional aggression-related cognitive, emotional, and behavioral outcomes. Outcomes include more positive attitudes toward violence, increased use of aggressive words or solutions to hypothetical problems, quicker recognition of facial anger, increased self-perception as being aggressive, increased feelings of anger and revenge motives, decreased sensitivity to scenes and images of real violence, and changes in brain function associated with lower executive control and heightened emotion.

Media Violence Is a Risk Factor for Violent Behavior

The research evidence shows clearly that media violence is a causal risk factor for aggressive and violent behavior. There is considerably less evidence concerning violent crimes, but the few cross-sectional and longitudinal studies that included violent crime measures also found similar links with media violence. The size of the media violence effect is as large as or larger than that of many factors commonly accepted by public policymakers and the general public as valid risk factors for violent behavior.... [Several] studies have directly compared video game and TV violence using the same participants and the same measures; they generally find a somewhat larger effect for video games. Thus, we expect that the effect of violent video games on long-term violence will be larger than that of TV violence and smaller than that of gang membership. Furthermore, it is likely that overall media violence exposure has a somewhat larger effect than any individual type of media violence. In any case, the figure makes clear that media violence exposure has a larger effect on later violent behavior than does substance use, abusive parents, poverty, living in a broken home, or having low IQ.

Watching Violent Movies Encourages Teenagers to Drink Alcohol

Society for Prevention Research

The Society for Prevention Research is an international member-ship organization that focuses on programs and policies con-cerned with the prevention of social, physical, and mental health problems and the promotion of health, safety, and well being.

R-rated movies portray violence and other behaviors deemed inappropriate for children under 17 year of age. A new study finds one more reason why parents should not let their kids watch those movies: adolescents who watch R-rated movies are more likely to try alcohol at a young age.

Published in the March [2010] issue of *Prevention Science*, a scientific journal of the Society for Prevention Research, the study of 6,255 children examined the relationship between watching R-rated movies and the probability of alcohol use across different levels of "sensation seeking," which is a ten-dency to seek out risky experiences. The study was funded by the National Institute on Alcohol Abuse and Alcoholism and conducted by James D. Sargent, MD, a pediatrician at Dart-mouth Medical School. The children were surveyed every 8 months for a period of two years from 2003 through 2005.

"The study found that watching R-rated movies affected the level of sensation seeking among adolescents. It showed that R-rated movies not only contain scenes of alcohol use that prompt adolescents to drink, they also jack up the sensa-tion seeking tendency, which makes adolescents more prone to engage in all sorts of risky behaviors" Sargent said.

"There is another take home point in the findings. When it comes to the direct effect on alcohol use, the influence of R-rated movies depends on sensation seeking level. High sensation seekers are already at high risk for use of alcohol, and watching a lot of R-rated movies raises their risk only a little. But for low sensation seekers, R-rated movies make a big difference. In fact, exposure to R-rated movies can make a low sensation seeking adolescent drink like a high sensation seeking adolescent," Sargent explained.

The Dartmouth pediatrician said that one possible explanation is high sensation seeking adolescents tend to get their experiences out on the street. They hang around other high sensation seekers, who are also engaging in risky behaviors, so there is less room for movies to make a difference in their risk for alcohol use.

R-rated Movies and Alcohol

"The message to parents is clear. Take the movie ratings literally. Under 17 should not be permitted to see R-rated movies," Sargent said.

The study was based on telephone surveys of 6,522 adolescents aged 10–14 years. Parental consent and adolescent consent was obtained prior to interviewing each respondent. To protect confidentiality, adolescents indicated their answers to sensitive questions by pressing numbers on the telephone, rather than speaking aloud. The study sample mirrored the U.S. adolescent population with respect to age, sex, household income and census region, but with a slightly higher percentage of Hispanics and a slightly lower percentage of Blacks.

Sensation seeking was based on how individual subjects identified with statements like: "I like to do scary things, I like to do dangerous things, I often think there is nothing to do, and I like to listen to loud music." Adolescents were also asked if they had ever tried alcohol that their parents were not aware of. This excluded adolescents who initiated drinking with sips of alcohol provided by parents. R-rated movie watching was measured by asking respondents if they had watched a random selection of movie titles drawn from box office hits during 2003 that had grossed at least $15 million. The movie titles included movies that had G (general audience), P/G (parental guidance) and R (restricted) ratings.

Taming Baby Rage: Why Are Some Kids So Angry?

Nikhil Swaminathan

Nikhil Swaminathan is a writer for Scientific American.

It is not the cartoons that make your kids smack playmates or violently grab their toys but, rather, a lack of social skills, according to new research.

A Genetic Link to Violent Behavior

"It's a natural behavior and it's surprising that the idea that children and adolescents learn aggression from the media is still relevant," says Richard Tremblay, a professor of pediatrics, psychiatry and psychology at the University of Montreal, who has spent more than two decades tracking 35,000 Canadian children (from age five months through their 20s) in search of the roots of physical aggression. "Clearly youth were violent before television appeared."

Tremblay's previous results have suggested that children on average reach a peak of violent behavior (biting, scratching, screaming, hitting . . .) around 18 months of age. The level of aggression begins to taper between the ages of two and five as they begin to learn other, more sophisticated ways of communicating their needs and wants.

Tremblay on Wednesday [October 17, 2007] is set to present preliminary study results showing a genetic signature consistent with chronic violent behavior at a meeting of The Royal Society, the U.K.'s [United Kingdom's] academy of science, in London.

"We're looking at to what extent the chronically aggressive individuals show differences in terms of gene expressions compared to those on the normal trajectory," he told ScientificAmerican.com. "The individuals that are chronically aggressive have . . . more genes that are not expressed." The fact that a gene can be silenced or the level of protein it encodes reduced, he added, "is an indication that the problem is at a very basic level."

Damaged genes may make it hard for children to acquire language, frustrating them and making them prone to violence, among other means of making themselves heard.

When children first begin to poke, prod and even slap, parents, teachers and siblings often react by indicating that those behaviors are inappropriate. But, citing studies done in animals, Tremblay notes that an unfit environment beginning in the womb may affect a child's ability to learn this lesson in the first place. And he plans to extend his genetic studies to include expectant mothers to determine if their behavior during pregnancy is linked to the down tuning of genes that may be associated with chronic aggression.

"In the long studies we've been doing, we've measured a number of characteristics during pregnancy and after birth that are good predictors" of chronic aggression in children, Tremblay notes. Possible factors that might influence neurobiological development of the fetus, he says, include smoking, drinking, poor nutrition and excessive stress.

Tremblay speculates that genes play a significant role: for instance damaged genes may make it hard for children to acquire language, frustrating them and making them prone to violence, among other means of making themselves heard. "When you don't master language," Tremblay says, "it's hard to get people to understand what you want."

Kate Keenan, an associate professor of psychiatry at the University of Chicago, views this new genetic analysis as the logical next step in Tremblay's long-term exploration into childhood aggression. She believes Tremblay's work may help uncover genetic profiles distinct to chronically aggressive children that may allow researchers to answer questions like, "Can we differentiate [between these kids] even earlier?" [and] "How early can you intervene?"

Violence in the Media Has No Negative Effect on the General Population

Tom Grimes, James A. Anderson, and Lori Bergen

Tom Grimes is a professor of journalism and mass communication at Texas State University; James A. Anderson is a professor of communication at the University of Utah; and Lori Bergen is professor and director of the school of journalism and mass communication at Texas State University.

Ludwig Wittgenstein, the 20th-century Austrian/English philosopher, provided an intellectual legacy that, frankly, only professional philosophers can understand. He was a logician who applied tediously crafted principles of logic to the formation of language, among other study areas, in philosophy.

Wittgenstein did distinguish himself, however, in one way that everyone can understand. In the late 1920s and early 1930s, when his work was at its most influential—when an entire philosophical movement, logical positivism, was building around it—he renounced the work he had produced up to that point, claiming he had made serious logical errors. He eventually introduced work that addressed those errors. Our point is that his faithfulness to the truth, no matter how much reputational damage he sustained, still stands, in all its power, as one of Wittgenstein's lasting moral and intellectual achievements.

We are not comparing ourselves to the great Wittgenstein, of course. But we stand ready to renounce, in the twinkle of an eye, what we advocate here when, or if, empirical evidence surfaces that reasonable men and women would consider a credible refutation of our position. Indeed, we *hope* our arguments in this book motivate our critics to prove us wrong. If they can do that then don't we all benefit? An early reviewer of this text called this claim into question (actually she or he called it bull****), but it is at the heart of Karl Popper's critical rationalism [in *The Logic of Scientific Discovery*], which describes how science should advance. The literature of media effects research provides convincing evidence of its authors' attempts to silence critics and suppress alternative voices even to the extent of telling us not to believe ourselves. Here's what we mean. [G.G.] Sparks, in an attempt to explain why it may not appear to some that media violence provokes social aggression, states,

> One possibility is that the conclusion from personal experience is valid for one-self but not for others. The fact that violent media might not trigger aggressive behavior for one individual does not necessarily mean that media violence functions the same way for everyone. Another possibility is that one's impression about being invulnerable to media impact is simply incorrect. Perhaps the effects of media violence are difficult for people to detect in themselves—even though the effects are definitely present.

Media content does not determine the use children and adults will make of it.

Foundational Principles

Both of those possibilities may even be possible, but the argument serves to bulletproof the body of media effects research from the questions of the rational, reflective individual. We hope you will consider these two possibilities in light of your own experience and perhaps those of your children or of your childhood.

The writing here is easily recognized as contrarian (we like to think of it as skeptical realism), but it is not without its own position. From our over 100 years of collective work in media and media effects, *we hold to the following to be true*:

- Media effects exist. They are multiple and manifest. Even the choice to watch or read something is a media effect.

- Children and adults *can* use media in ways that result in personal and societal harm. That is, if there is an intent to harm someone through manipulation of a media message, it likely can be done.

- Media content does not determine the use children and adults will make of it. That is, the simple fact that violent media content exists doesn't, in itself, have any important meaning. Viewers must *do* something with that content.

- Media content works through interpretation, and interpretation begins in physiology, moves through cognitive processes, but in the end relies on social processes for its consequences.

- The presence of violence in our media may present a potential for "doing something about it/to stop it/to censor it." However, whether we, as a society, decide to censor it or whatever depends on various social processes that interact with violent media content, not on simple exposure to the content in and of itself.

- The way we behave does not develop independently of the social processes that provide for the development and sustain the behavior once learned.

- Certain well-recognized, catalogued mental illnesses most likely account for the majority of the correlational data that claim media violence causes behavioral aggression.

- The layperson can reliably consult his or her own experience with the media, but as with all examinations of one's own life, it requires systematic effort.

- There is a rich panoply of theory that goes beyond strict, narrow, and technical psychological explanations that should be used to develop policy for children and the media.

- Much of what passes as recommendations for policy is fear-mongering.

- Much traditional media effects research is a party—perhaps unwitting, perhaps not—to a political process that holds out simple solutions to social problems that do not involve a restructuring of privilege.

- The commitment to adequate resources to social justice, economic opportunity, and educational equality is the first and most effective line of defense against violence in society.

It is not true that banning content will reduce violence, social aggression, and incivility in society.

There are also some points that must be intercepted as false. *We hold the following to be false:*

- It is not true that exposure is all that is necessary for a life-forming effect to occur.

- It is not true that theory that explains the empirical findings is well developed and provides a good understanding of how exposure works.

- It is not true that our rejection—or anyone's rejection—of models built exclusively on media exposure (i.e., mere exposure can result in psychological harm/increases of aggression in society) is not the same as claiming that there are no effects.

- It is not true that there are no useful theories of media effects other than narrowly focused psychological explanations.

- It is not true that all children are at risk from the media.

- It is not true that banning content will reduce violence, social aggression, and incivility in society.

- It is not true that the layperson cannot recognize the effect or lack thereof of media exposure in his or her own life.

- It is not true that the interventions proposed to break whatever connection exists between exposure to media violence and aggression/psychological harm in society are simple to implement, are without predictable harms, and will have no unintended consequences.

- It is not true that media violence research is the only objectively conducted science that is independent of politics, devoid of moralizing, and free from class-based ideology.

The Research Linking Media Violence to Aggression Is Weak and Ambiguous

Free Expression Policy Project

The Free Expression Policy Project provides research and advocacy on free speech, copyright, and media democracy issues.

This Fact Sheet answers some frequently-asked questions about social science research into the effects of media violence. The bottom line is that despite the claims of some psychologists and politicians, the actual research results have been weak and ambiguous.

This should not be surprising: media violence is so pervasive in our lives, and comes in so many different contexts and styles, that it is impossible to make accurate generalizations about its real-world effects based on experiments in a laboratory, or on studies that simply find statistical correlations between media-viewing and aggressive behavior.

Of course, the First Amendment would be a significant barrier to censoring violent images and ideas even if social science had in fact produced statistical evidence of adverse effects. But it is important for the ongoing debate on this issue that the real facts about media violence studies are understood.

- No one seriously doubts that the mass media have profound effects on our attitudes and behavior. But the effects vary tremendously, depending on the different ways that media content is presented, and the personality, background, intelligence, and life experience of the viewer.

There Is No Proof That Media Violence Causes Aggression

- Although many people believe that media violence causes aggression, it's doubtful that this can ever be proved by the methods of social science. For one thing, violent images and ideas come in too many different styles and contexts for researchers to be able to make meaningful generalizations about effects.

- Somewhere between 200 and 300 laboratory experiments, field studies, and correlational studies have been done on media violence (not thousands, as some activists have claimed), and their results are dubious and inconsistent. In some cases, experimenters have manipulated disappointing results until they came up with at least one positive finding; then proclaimed that the experiment supported their hypothesis that media violence causes aggression. Some experiments have found more aggressive behavior after viewing nonviolent shows like *Sesame Street* and *Mr. Rogers' Neighborhood*.

- Professor Jonathan Freedman of the University of Toronto, an independent expert who reviewed the media violence literature in the 1980s, concluded that the research did not "provide either strong or consistent support for the hypothesis that exposure to media violence causes aggression or crime. Rather, the results have been extremely inconsistent and weak." Updating his resarch in 2002, Freedman reported that fewer than half the studies support a causal effect.

- For the minority of experiments that have yielded positive results, the explanation probably has more to do with the general arousal effect of violent entertainment than with viewers actually imitating violent acts. Laboratory experiments, moreover, do not measure real aggression but other behaviors that the researchers consider "proxies" for real aggression—popping balloons, giving noise blasts, hitting Bobo dolls, or other forms of aggressive play.

- Laboratory experiments also suffer from "experimenter demand effect"—subjects responding to what they think the researcher wants. They know that behavior is permitted in the lab that would be unacceptable in the real world.

- Because of the weakness of laboratory experiments in predicting behavior, psychologists have undertaken "field experiments" that more accurately replicate the real world. Freedman reported that the overwhelming majority of field experiments found no adverse effects on behavior from exposure to media violence.

It's . . . likely that our fascination with violence satisfies some basic human needs.

- Some correlational studies show a "link" or "association" between the subjects' amount of violent TV viewing and real-world aggressive behavior. But a link or association does not establish causation. It is likely that a combination of factors (level of intelligence, education, social background and attitudes, genetic predisposition, and economic status) account for both the entertainment preferences and the behavior.

- Some correlational studies do not even focus on violent TV but simply examine overall amount of television viewing. This reinforces the probability that people whose cultural and activity choices are limited and who thus watch excessive amounts of TV also may have a more limited range of responses to conflict situations.

Nonviolent People Like Violent Entertainment

- Violence has been a subject in literature and the arts since the beginning of human civilization. In part, this simply reflects the unfortunate realities of the world. But it's also likely that our fascination with violence satisfies some basic human needs. The adrenalin rush, the satisfactions of imagination, fantasy, and vicarious adventure, probably explain why millions of nonviolent people enjoy violent entertainment.

- Because the mass media presents violence in so many different ways (news, sports, action movies, cartoons, horror movies, documentaries, war stories with pacifist themes), it is particularly difficult to generalize about its impact. Even social scientists who believe that violent entertainment has adverse effects don't agree on what kinds of violent images or ideas are harmful. Some point to cartoons; others point to movies in which a violent hero is rewarded; others fault the gory focus of television news.

- Every federal appellate court that has addressed the issue has rejected the claim that social science research shows adverse effects from violent content in entertainment. In a June 2011 decision striking down a law that restricted minors' access to violent video games, the Supreme Court noted that research studies "do not prove that violent video games *cause* minors to *act* aggressively (which would at least be a beginning)." Instead, "nearly all of the research is based on correlation, not evidence of causation, and most of the studies suffer from significant, admitted flaws in methodology.... They show at best some correlation between exposure to violent entertainment and minuscule real-world effects, such as children's feeling more aggressive or making louder noises in the few minutes after playing a violent game than after playing a nonviolent game."

- There have been instances where criminals or others engaged in violent behavior have imitated specific aspects of a violent movie or TV show. But the fact that millions of other viewers have not engaged in imitation suggests that predisposition is the important factor, and that if the bad actors had not seen that particular movie or show, they would have imitated something else. It is impossible to predict which episodes or descriptions will be imitated by unstable individuals, and equally impossible to ban every book, movie, magazine article, song, game, or other cultural product that somebody might imitate.

- There is much that is pernicious, banal, and crude in popular culture—not all of it violent. The best ways to address concerns about bad media messages of all types are media literacy education, prompt attention to danger signs for violent behavior in schools, workplaces, and other venues, and increased funding for creative, educational, nonviolent TV programming.

CHAPTER 3

Are Violent Video Games Harmful?

Overview: There Are Benefits as Well as Dangers from Video Games

Bill Jenkins

Bill Jenkins holds a Ph.D. in psychobiology from Florida State University, and is one of the founders and contributers of The Science of Learning Blog.

We've all seen the news reports, but how do video games really affect the brain? The short answer is this: researchers are working on it. While a great many studies have been done, science has a long way to go before we fully understand the impact video games can have.

The brain is a malleable, "plastic" structure that can change and evolve with every stimulus we give it. Whether that stimulus comes from listening to Tchaikovsky [Russian composer], studying Spanish, training in karate, or jumping through the mushroom kingdom in Super Mario Bros. Wii [video game], every single input can affect the wiring of the brain if the conditions are right.

In a December 2011 article in *Nature Reviews Neuroscience*, six experts in neuroscience and cognitive psychology—Daphne Bavelier, C. Shawn Green, Doug Hyun Han, Perry F. Renshaw, Michael M. Merzenich and Douglas A. Gentile—offer their perspectives on frequently asked questions related to the effects of video games on the brain:

Are there beneficial effects of video games? Does evidence point to improvements in cognitive function?

Given the wide variety of game types and the tasks they demand of the brain, this is an extremely complex and layered issue. Han and Renshaw cite studies indicating that game play may improve visual-spatial capacity, visual acuity, task switching, decision making and object tracking. In perception, gaming has been shown to enhance low-level vision, visual attention, processing speed and statistical inference. These skills are not necessarily general improvements in cognitive functioning, but specific skills transferrable to similar tasks.

Does playing video games have negative effects on the brain and behavior?

On this issue, the jury is essentially unanimous: intensive play of high-action games has been shown to have negative cognitive effects. Merzenich references studies that indicate such games can create "listlessness and discontent in slower-paced and less stimulating academic, work or social environments." Research has drawn connections between playing more violent games and an increase in more aggressive thoughts. Games with anti-social or violent content "have been shown to reduce empathy, to reduce stress associated with observing or initiating anti-social actions, and to increase confrontational and disruptive behaviors in the real world."

How strong is the evidence that video games are addictive?

While strong evidence is mounting, research is proceeding but still incomplete. According to Han and Renshaw, investigations suggest that "brain areas that respond to game stimuli in patients with on-line game addiction are similar to those that respond to drug cue-induced craving in patients with substance dependence." In addition, they state that gaming dependence has been shown to create "dysfunction in five domains: academic, social, occupational, developmental and behavioral." While gaming addiction may differ from other types of addiction, it clearly appears to be a very real issue.

What should the role of video games be in education and rehabilitation?

Again, if we come back to the underlying fact that any stimulus can change the brain under the right conditions, video games—a source of stimuli—certainly have a role to play in these areas. The question is, what stimuli are beneficial to which individuals, and how can we customize the gaming experience to give the learner or patient the stimuli that they most need at a given moment? Adaptive technologies that track a user's responses and present follow-up material based on those response patterns, especially when wielded by an experienced educator or clinician, offer immense potential.

Where is neuroscience headed in this field?

Clearly, studies have shown that video games affect and change the brain, both for ill as well as for good. Some researchers, such as neuroscientist Paul Howard-Jones of Bristol University, are already experimenting with ways to harness computer gaming to enhance classroom learning. Future studies are likely to uncover both detrimental effects of video games and significant benefits of their employment as learning and rehabilitation tools.

"Because of their great didactic efficiencies," says Merzenich, "and because of brain plasticity-based exercises can improve the performance characteristics of the brain of almost every child, these new game-like tools shall be at the core of a schooling revolution."

The Demise of Guys': How Video Games and Porn Are Ruining a Generation

Philip G. Zimbardo and Nikita Duncan

Philip G. Zimbardo is a professor emeritus at Stanford University noted for his groundbreaking work on the Stanford prison experiment. Nikita Duncan is an artist and psychologist. They are the authors of The Demise of Guys: Why Boys Are Struggling and What We Can Do About It.

Is the overuse of video games and pervasiveness of online porn causing the demise of guys?

Increasingly, researchers say yes, as young men become hooked on arousal, sacrificing their school work and relationships in the pursuit of getting a tech-based buzz.

Young Men Hooked on Arousal Have Trouble Dealing with Life

Every compulsive gambler, alcoholic or drug addict will tell you that they want increasingly more of a game or drink or drug in order to get the same quality of buzz.

Video game and porn addictions are different. They are "arousal addictions," where the attraction is in the novelty, the variety or the surprise factor of the content. Sameness is soon habituated; newness heightens excitement. In traditional drug arousal, conversely, addicts want more of the same cocaine or heroin or favorite food.

The consequences could be dramatic: The excessive use of video games and online porn in pursuit of the next thing is creating a generation of risk-averse guys who are unable (and unwilling) to navigate the complexities and risks inherent to real-life relationships, school and employment.

Stories about this degeneration are rampant: In 2005, Seungseob Lee, a South Korean man, went into cardiac arrest after playing "StarCraft" for nearly 50 continuous hours. In 2009, MTV's "True Life" highlighted the story of a man named Adam whose wife kicked him out of their home—they have four kids together—because he couldn't stop watching porn.

Norwegian mass murder suspect Anders Behring Breivik reported during his trial that he prepared his mind and body for his marksman-focused shooting of 77 people by playing "World of Warcraft" for a year and then "Call of Duty" for 16 hours a day.

Research into this area goes back a half-century.

In 1954, researchers Peter Milner and James Olds discovered the pleasure center of the brain. In their experiments, an electrical current was sent to the limbic system of a rat's brain whenever it moved to a certain area of its cage. The limbic sytem is a portion of the brain that controls things like emotion, behavior and memory. The researchers hypothesized that if the stimulation to the limbic system were unpleasant, the rats would stay away from that part of the cage.

Surprisingly, the rats returned to that portion of the cage again and again, despite the sensation.

Video games . . . go wrong when the person playing them is desensitized to reality and real-life interactions with others.

In later experiments, when they were allowed to push a stimulation lever on their own accord, they self-stimulated hundreds of times per hour. Even when given the option to eat when hungry or to stimulate the pleasure center, the rats chose the stimulation until they were physically exhausted and on the brink of death.

This new kind of human addictive arousal traps users into an expanded present hedonistic time zone. Past and future are distant and remote as the present moment expands to dominate everything. That present scene is totally dynamic, with images changing constantly.

A recent study from the Centers for Disease Control and Prevention found that "regular porn users are more likely to report depression and poor physical health than nonusers are. . . . The reason is that porn may start a cycle of isolation. . . . Porn may become a substitute for healthy face-to-face interactions, social or sexual."

Similarly, video games also go wrong when the person playing them is desensitized to reality and real-life interactions with others.

Violence in video games is often synonymous with success. Children with more of a propensity for aggression are more attracted to violent video media, but violent media, in turn, can also make them more aggressive. This could be related to the fact that most video games reward players for violent acts, often permitting them to move to the next level in a game.

Yet research reported in the *Annual Review of Public Health* suggests a link between violent video games and real-life aggression: Given the opportunity, both adults and children were more aggressive after playing violent games. And people who identify themselves with violent perpetrators in video games are able to take aggressive action while playing that role, reinforcing aggressive behavior.

Young men—who play video games and use porn the most—are being digitally rewired in a totally new way that demands constant stimulation. And those delicate, developing brains are being catered to by video games and porn-on-demand, with a click of the mouse, in endless variety.

Such new brains are also totally out of sync in traditional school classes, which are analog, static and interactively passive. Academics are based on applying past lessons to future problems, on planning, on delaying gratifications, on work coming before play and on long-term goal-setting.

Guys are also totally out of sync in romantic relationships, which tend to build gradually and subtly, and require interaction, sharing, developing trust and suppression of lust at least until "the time is right."

Less extreme cases of arousal addiction may go unnoticed or be diagnosed as an attention or mood disorder. But we are in a national, and perhaps global, Guy Disaster Mode that needs to be noticed and solutions advanced to fix a totally novel phenomenon, which will only increase in intensity and breadth without the concerted efforts of educators, gamemakers, parents, guys and gals.

It's time to press play and get started reversing these trends.

Violent Video Games Change Young Men's Brainwaves

Rupert Shepherd

Rupert Shepherd is a writer for Medical News Today.

The annual meeting of the Radiological Society of North America (RSNA) was presented with a study made of the brain of young men, using fMRI scans (functional magnetic resonance imaging). In as little as one week, regions of the brain associated with cognitive function and emotional control had noticeable changes.

Violent Video Games Alter the Brain

The arguments for and against video games have been going for as long as the games themselves, and even getting as far as the Supreme Court in 2010, but other than various statistics, there has never been any exact scientific or biological evidence that could be drawn on.

Yang Wang, M.D., assistant research professor in the Department of Radiology and Imaging Sciences at Indiana University School of Medicine in Indianapolis said:

> "For the first time, we have found that a sample of randomly assigned young adults showed less activation in certain frontal brain regions following a week of playing violent video games at home. . . . These brain regions are important for controlling emotion and aggressive behavior."

What the researchers did is take 22 healthy adult males, age 18 to 29, who were not avid game players in the past. The group was split and randomly assigned into two groups of 11.

Members of the first group were instructed to play a shooting video game for 10 hours at home for one week and refrain from playing the following week. The second group did not play a violent video game at all during the two-week period.

All 22 men were analysed with an fMRI scan at the beginning of the study and with follow-up exams at one and two weeks. During their examination the participants also completed an emotional interference task, pressing buttons according to the color of visually presented words. Words indicating violent actions were interspersed among nonviolent action words. In addition, the participants completed a cognitive inhibition counting task.

Violent video game play has a long-term effect on brain functioning.

After just one week of violent game play, the video game group members showed less activation in the left inferior frontal lobe during the emotional task and less activation in the anterior cingulate cortex during the counting task, compared to their baseline results and the results of the control group after one week. After the second week without game play, the changes to the executive regions of the brain were diminished.

You would have to wonder as well, if those who watch 10 hours of violent movies per week, might also exhibit a similar change in the brain.

Dr. Wang said:

> "These findings indicate that violent video game play has a long-term effect on brain functioning."

Michael Lipton, MD, PhD, of Albert Einstein College of Medicine in New York, who was not involved in the study, called the findings preliminary, and that he's not necessarily surprised by them.

"There have been a lot of studies that expose patients to novel behaviors, and you see changes in brain activity that then go away over time. . . . The problem is, how does that translate into real world functionality?"

Violent Video Games Influence Children to Kill

Flare

Flare *is a Canadian fashion magazine.*

"Come on, finish your work quickly, or the toy shop will close," said mum. "I will break the door of the toy shop," replied her four-year-old son.

"You are not that strong, you don't even eat properly," she smiled.

"I have special powers. I even have a gun and a sword."

Mum was no longer amused. "What special powers? And what would you do with the gun and sword?"

"I can change my appearance, grab the shopkeeper and shoot him. There will be blood on his body and he will die. Then I will take all the toys."

"But good people don't hurt anyone."

"Yes, they do. Good people kill bad people, like Obi Wun and Darth Vedar."

This kind of conversation between mother and child isn't unusual for me. Of late I have been approached more and more by distraught mothers complaining of a growing display of aggressive behaviour by their children. Words like hitting, killing, shooting, murder, fire, punch, death, blood have become a part of children's everyday vocabulary. The games children play, their hobbies, their toys, the books they read, especially amongst boys, have changed alarmingly. Very few are interested in Snakes and Ladders, Bingo, Scrabble, Candyland, hide and seek. These games are now considered boring.

If children are left unsupervised on play dates, their favourite pastime is interactive violent video games.

While girls might still be collecting ornaments and dresses for their Barbies, boys are busy collecting guns, swords and gadgets that are shown in these games to inflict harm upon "the enemy." As girls add Princess tales and Hannah Montana to their reading collection, boys prefer *Ben Ten*, *Harry Potter*, *Star Wars*, *Hulk* and *Mask*. In short, they are spending much more time playing interactive video games, 90 per cent of them violent. It is instructive to study the downside of technology, especially technology that our children are using without supervision. During the last two decades video games have emerged as one of the most popular forms of entertainment among children and adolescents.

The message being learnt is that it is "all right" to kill.

The opportunities for them to learn; the resources at their fingertips are hard to fathom.

The World Wide Web is like a vast, almost limitless encyclopaedia, unlike *Encyclopaedia Britannica*, they talk to it and it talks back. So it is especially disconcerting to see armies of these very kids, mutilating and killing everyone in their path—and having a great time doing it. It's the dark side of heightened technology, but one to which we ought to pay close attention to.

What is alarming is the fact that the one who kills the most is the "Hero". The more you kill, the more rewards you get. The message being learnt is that it is "all right" to kill. In order to be a hero, you should have the power to kill. In the last few years, manufacturers have made these games so close to life that children have started dressing and pretending like these characters, personifying them as heroes in their daily lives. Exposure to violence has desensitised them. There is no feeling of remorse when they hit or hurt somebody, they don't feel anything. The use of aggression is becoming common and display of violence over trivial issues is increasing.

Scientists and researchers, who were warning us against the harmful effects of watching too much television, are alarmed at the present situation. Television is two-dimensional and isn't conducive to learning in the same way, but this three-dimensional interactive technology gives the children a hands-on experience. And what are they learning—precision in killing.

These violent video games are more popular amongst teenagers. David Grossman again mentions in his book that some of these games closely resemble military marksmanship training devices. Both teach the user to hit a target, both help rehearse the act of killing, both come complete with guns that have recoil—the side slams back when the trigger is pulled. No one wants to see these devices in the hands of civilians.

The entire world is reaping the bitter harvest of this dark side of technology. We read news of students all over the world killing their teachers and girlfriends on trivial matters. In Pakistan, the administrators of high schools, colleges and universities are increasingly faced with the problem of aggression. This is not to say that interactive violent video games are the only reason for eruption of violence, but they are definitely playing a major role in desensitising children to violence. Imagine the damage a young boy who has practised these games for endless hours can inflict if a real weapon is given in his hand.

Life is no more sacred and weapons are within easy reach. Parents beware.

The Dubious Perils of Pac-Man

Timothy Maher

Timothy Maher is the assistant managing editor of Technology Review *magazine.*

2 8 Years Ago in TR [*Technology Review*].

One writer bristled at the idea that video games might be corrupting her daughters.

In 1982, Surgeon General C. Everett Koop warned an audience of public-health workers about the three top culprits for family violence: economic hardship, TV, and video games. "All you have to do," Koop said, "is see a youngster playing a video game and watch his behavior as exhibited by body language or outright attacks on components of the game or the television screen to understand just how deep is the connection."

Koop's words prompted a rebuttal—titled "Will Pac-Man Consume Our Nation's Youth?"—in the June 1983 issue of TR. Carolyn Meinel, a computing enthusiast and author of a book on hacking, said Koop might have had a point about TV and poverty, but he was dead wrong on video games. Koop's warnings on the hazards of explicit TV violence are documented by extensive research done during the 1960s and 1970s. . . . However, there is scant evidence to support Koop's assertions on the hazards of video games. Unlike TV, such games are typically highly symbolic with no actual portrayal of blood and guts. Like chess, the figures zapping one another on the video screen are stylistic images that bear little resemblance to human forms.

Of course, all those human forms that didn't exist in *Pac-Man* or *Defender* now exist in graphic, bloody detail in games like *Gears of War* and *Mortal Kombat*. But experts still debate whether that imagery is a harmless (if slightly depraved) emotional outlet or something that leads to aggression in the real world. (The same goes for the effects of TV violence, despite Meinel's assertion that the issue was settled.)

Meinel's feeling was that video games were here to stay whether we liked them or not—so we might as well use them as a tool for good.

> I first introduced my kids to computer games back in 1974.... The kids learned to add fractions by mixing chemicals to grow monsters on an orange phosphor screen.... I beam smugly when the neighborhood toddlers come over and my three-year-old Ginny runs to the computer and loads a game of *Breakout* for them to play. Valerie, nearly five now, uses the screen editor to work on spelling.

While there have been a fair number of studies on the topic [of the hazards of video games], none have been definitive enough to settle the debate among policy makers and social scientists.

Meinel saw the outrage against video games on a continuum of outrage against any youth sensation and contended that the real target was the kids themselves.

> In an attempt to reverse this trend, state legislators in New York introduced a bill last year to ban the banning of video games—to the applause of chronic adolescents such as me.... Why doesn't the surgeon general warn us that the kid who forks a queen with a rook today will be holding the principal and the playground monitor hostage with a zip gun tomorrow?

Meinel, now a freelance journalist living in New Mexico, says her daughters, who are in their 30s and 40s, show no detrimental effects from the activities of their youth. "None of them has a police record," she says.

She's aware that games have gotten much more graphic and violent in the nearly three decades since she wrote the article, but she laments the fact that people are still quibbling over their effects (in June of this year [2011], for instance, the U.S. Supreme Court struck down a California law banning the sale of violent games to children). While there have been a fair number of studies on the topic, none have been definitive enough to settle the debate among policy makers and social scientists.

"What if it turned out that graphically violent computer games provided a safe release so that I don't have to worry—as a 65-year-old woman walking around in the middle of nowhere on a hike or something—about some crazed guy jumping out of a bush with a chain saw?" she says. "What if that were the outcome, that these games prevent violence? It's worth finding out."

Athwart: To Save the Dead-Eyed Child?

James Lileks

James Lileks is a journalist, columnist, blogger, and the author of Mommy Knows Worst: Highlights from the Golden Age of Bad Parenting Advice.

While the dead-eyed child squirms in your hands, piteously begging to be freed, the voice in your head gives you a choice: kill it, or save it. You suspect there will be consequences either way.

That's a scenario in the video game *BioShock*, and you can imagine the outrage: This is entertainment? What sort of culture produces such depravity? Perhaps this will help: The child is possessed by a drug-induced insanity, she's accompanied by a lumbering robot that wants to kill you, you're in a ruined underwater city populated by people driven mad by genetic manipulation, and the entire story is about a society constructed along the principles of Ayn Rand.

Hope that helps. If not, play the game. *BioShock* rewards your humanity, plays with your loyalties, picks apart your character's sanity. It's a way of telling a story that some hesitate to call Art, because unlike Tolstoy, you can shoot fireballs from your hand. But for the kids who grew up controlling digital alter egos, it's high literature—and was probably illegal for minors in California. Until the courts weighed in.

Late in June the Supremes struck down a California law that said it shall be illegal to sell, rent, describe, admit the existence of, or otherwise disseminate a violent video game to minors, even if they can join the Army after their birthday tomorrow and get a serious gun with actual bullets. The decision contained lots of solid eye-glazing constitutional folderol, most of which confounds parents who wonder why it shouldn't be illegal to sell a ten-year-old *StrangleFest Death Party*. (But Mom! The controller vibrates to simulate the death throes of your victims! Timmy has it! Pleeeeeze!) Shouldn't the Supreme Court take on real issues, like whether protected speech includes marching right down to the store that sold your kid the horrible game and giving them a piece of your mind?

Some on the right liked the pushback of a speech-regulating law; others worried about the kinder-kulture coarseness of shoot-'em-ups. Either way, you can't say it was a glib decision: The Court noted that literature abounds with violence, citing some torture-porn from Homer. This might be relevant if kids were playing Homer simulators. But reading is not doing; watching is not doing. Games are kinetic entertainment activities, if you will. They're spellbinding and immersive. There will always be those who see such statutes in the continuum of hapless prudery: Why, back in the 19th century, there were laws preventing an adult from describing a bout of fisticuffs with semaphore flags if there was a minor present. That comstockery was struck down by the courts, too. Same thing here. But not really.

Today's games contain much more realistic depictions of ballistic perforations. "Realism," however, is a shifting standard. In the mid-1990s, which is two geological ages ago in gamer terms, there was "controversy" over *Doom*, which now looks like you're fighting off angry pieces of Lego. *Duke Nukem* provided a ration of hysteria when someone heard from someone else that the player could shoot strippers. Ink was spilled like blood in the last reel of a Peckinpah film, condemning this new low, but it missed the point. You could shoot anything in the game. If, however, you hit what we call in the post-Weiner era a "featured dancer," you would be swarmed by policemen who had been mutated into bipedal hogs by space aliens, and you would die. It was the game's way of establishing a moral code.

Yes, that sounds silly. You like to think that all your parenting instilled the "don't shoot the strippers" lesson early on, if only by the behavior you modeled. But then a gamer of a certain age hears about games like *Grand Theft Auto*, which most disapproving press accounts describe as a sociopathic instruction kit on the best way to apply a tire iron to a streetwalker, and the gamer yearns for the old days when there were codes of honor.

Does there have to be a law, for heaven's sake?

Oh, for the simple Manichean duality of *Pong*! Then *Pac-Man* ruined everything by making us seek the fruit at the expense of our own safety. That's when it all fell apart.

If games weren't the primary daily entertainment option for millions of minor boys, it might not be an issue. But concern over a few bad games vilifies titles like *L.A. Noire*—you're a cop in a [Raymond] Chandler world—or the sprawling western *Red Dead Redemption*. Not for the Pooh set, but if they're off-limits to a 16-year-old, then so's a Road Runner cartoon.

Basic kvetch: Does there have to be a law, for heaven's sake? When you have a law that says kids can't buy the game, but shall borrow a friend's copy on the sly, then you get rulings that establish a minor's free-speech right to *Grand Theft Auto*, which means you'll have a kid sue his parents because they didn't give him Chainsaw Bob Orphanage Fracas IV for Christmas. It's not hard for parents to find out what a game's about, thanks to this thing called "the Internet." They might be alarmed to learn there's also a popular game in which small children are encouraged to imprison creatures in cramped, dark spheres, letting them out only to battle in cockfights that often send one to the hospital. Michael Vick got put away for something like that.

The game goes by the name of *Pokemon*.

By the way, if you release the child in *BioShock*, you get all sorts of rewards. Never met a gamer who didn't let the kid go.

Research Reporting Adverse Effects of Violent Video Games Is Flawed and Possibly Biased

John Walker

John Walker is a blogger, writer, and critic.

A number of people have got in touch to let us know about a new study that has been published, identifying once again that violent videogames may have an effect on the brain of the player. It's a finding that, in general, is worth taking notice of—last week [the week of November 20, 2011] I wrote about a meta-analysis discussion conducted by *Nature* that showed a consensus amongst researchers that there is a noticeable change in the brain after prolongued exposure to violent videogames. However, things get more interesting when you dig into who was funding it. Which turns out to be a campaign group who have some dubious claims of their own. . . .

Research Misstates the Facts

[Functional magnetic resonance imaging scans] fMRIs were carried out before the study, one week in, and at the end of the second week, during which they completed an "emotional interference task", which involves pressing buttons according to the colour of visually presented words, as well as a cognitive inhibition counting task. Whatever those might be. The results of this demonstrated that those who were playing the violent videogames showed less activation in the left inferior frontal lobe for the emotional task, and less activation in the anterior cingulate cortex for the counting task, than those who had been weaving daisies into their hair for a week. A week later, after neither group had been playing games, the game playing gang saw diminished effects.

Dr Yang Wang of the research department [stated], somewhat confusingly, "These findings indicate that violent video game play has a long-term effect on brain functioning." Because the results, to my layman's eye, would indicate they have a short-term effect.

It's important to note a couple of things. Firstly, these results showed changes in regions of the brain, but absolutely did not show that the individuals involved demonstrated any violent or aggressive behaviour. These are regions of the brain associated with aggression and violence, and the results appear to show that violent videogames *are* affecting those regions. It's noteworthy, and clearly something that should grab our attention.... However, it is not, as newspapers like the *Daily Mail* of course leapt to conclude, that violent games "DO make people aggressive", as their rather defiant headline put it....

Funding Source Has Its Own Agenda

[When] you see a story like this, it's always worth looking at where the funding came from. And this time it was from a group called The Center For Successful Parenting, whose stated goal is "to help parents understand the consequences of our children viewing video violence". Which might suggest they've already rather made their minds up. But of course they could be a science-focused, results-based organisation. But, well, that slightly falls down at the first hurdle, when you look at their "NEWS UPDATES" section, which impressively seems to begin in 1945.

"Television was introduced in 1945

From 1945 to 1974 homicides in the United States increased 93%"

Oh come on.

From 1900 to 1945 homicide rates in the US increased 400%! Based on those figures I'm claiming the arrival of television massively prevented homicide! And why do these figures mysteriously stop in 1974, despite the world having aged a little since then? Because since 1974 homicide rates in the US have rather awkwardly been falling. This isn't the sort of organisation I really want to be behind the scientific data I'm studying. (Also, as an aside, in their mission statement they explain that "Our culture used to protect the innocence of our children." Um, when was that exactly? I'm struggling to put my finger on that period in history when children were more protected than they are right now.)

I have nothing against parenting advocacy groups, who wish to protect children and educate others to do the same. However, when they spread spurious claims . . . there's a problem.

And who are The Center For Successful Parenting? Well, that's pretty hard to find out, since even their own terms of service and privacy policy links are just text on a jpg. They're a registered charity with a pretty impressive revenue stream. And beyond that their director is called Dr. Larry Ley, that's all I've been able to dig up. Attempts to contact them by their email address failed, as the address stated on their site appears to be invalid. But it's not the first time they've funded a study like this.

In 2005 a research group, featuring . . . Dr. Vincent P. Matthews . . . , published similar findings, also funded by the Center For Successful Parenting.

Then in 2006 a study demonstrating harmful effects on the brain found its way to the press, which just happened to have one Dr. Vincent P. Matthews at the helm, and, gosh, was funded by The Center For Successful Parenting. It might just be me, but I think I'm detecting a pattern.

Naturally I have nothing against parenting advocacy groups, who wish to protect children and educate others to do the same. However, when they spread spurious claims, obfuscate the facts, selectively pluck findings that match their agenda, and use sensationalist language like "brain washing" and "shocking" in reporting scientific findings, there's a problem.

Of course, their funding the research does not necessarily bias the research, there's no evidence to suggest that the research group are anything other than science-focused and pursuing the truth, and the findings to be revealed tomorrow [November 30, 2011] do appear to correlate to the consensus, that playing violent games has an effect on the brain. How serious that effect is, and how it may manifest, and what other less infamous activities may cause similar effects is not yet known, and without this information there's a limit to what we can conclude. I'm pursuing that angle, and speaking to researchers to find out more, as I believe it's one of the most important questions gamers should be asking, for themselves and for their children.

CHAPTER 4

How Should Society Respond to Violence in the Media?

Chapter Preface

Violence in the media is as pervasive as it is controversial. A 2010 study by the Kaiser Family Foundation found that young people (ages 8–18) spend seven-and-a-half hours a day, seven days a week, interacting with media, more time than they spend on any other activity besides sleeping. Of particular significance is the increase in these numbers, up by more than an hour a day from a decade ago. Very often, the media that children interact with depicts violence. Violent music videos make up approximately 15 percent of all music videos, according to Caroline Knorr of Common Sense Media, and cartoons depict approximately twenty violent acts each hour, states the American Academy of Child and Adolescent Psychiatry. The American Academy of Pediatrics claims that television programming as a whole depicts 812 acts of violence every hour, exposing the typical American child to more than two hundred thousand acts of violence by his or her eighteenth birthday. A sample of seventy-seven PG-13 films included 2,251 violent acts, according to researchers at the University of California, Los Angeles. Video games are the most violent media form of all, with 85 percent of all video games depicting violence, says Dave Munger in a blog post for the website Cognitive Daily.

Those concerned with the potential for harm stemming from exposure to violent media typically favor one of three remedies: government regulation, parental oversight, or media education. Government regulation is the most controversial of the three. Advocates of government regulation point to research linking violent television programs, movies, video games, music, and music videos to aggression. It is appropriate for government to intervene when a situation exists that could harm its citizens, and there is significant research indicating children may imitate the aggressive or violent behavior they are exposed to in the media, these advocates argue. Opponents to regulation contend that the research linking violence in the media to actual violent acts is inconclusive and flawed. The American Civil Liberties Union argues that defining in law what is excessively violent and potentially harmful to children is difficult. The "slippery slope" argument is also often used—once you let the government decide what forms of media are too violent for children, you place at risk other First Amendment freedoms.

Relying on parental oversight is a less controversial remedy. The Center for Media Literacy recommends that parents take five actions:

- Reduce their children's exposure to media violence by setting limits on how much time their children spend with media and what they watch and interact with.

- Change the impact of violent images by experiencing the media with their children and initiating a discussion about what they see.

- Explore alternatives to media that solve conflicts with violence.

- Talk to other parents and communicate their standards to those who spend time with their children.

- Get involved in the debate over media violence and communicate their concerns to media owners and elected officials.

Media education has often been overlooked as a tool to address violence in the media. The Center for Media Literacy believes that media literacy education can provide children and teens with the critical inquiry skills they need to make sound judgments about the media they interact with every day. The center has identified five ways that effective media literacy can help children and teens:

- Reduce exposure to violent media by educating parents and caregivers.

- Change the impact of violent images and make sure that children and teens know the difference between fantasy and reality.

- Offer alternatives to material that focuses on violence as the solution to interpersonal conflict.

- Provide context for the cultural, social, and political background surrounding the violent media.

- Promote informed and civil debate in schools, the media, and community about the issues surrounding violent media.

In the following chapter, sociologists and journalists provide their perspectives on the question "How Should Society Respond to Violence in the Media?"

Parents Need to Monitor Their Children's Media Habits

Florence Cherry and Jo Ann Zenger

Florence Cherry is with the department of human development and family studies at the New York state college of human ecology at Cornell University, and Jo Ann Zenger is a parent-to-parent coordinator at the Cornell Cooperative Extension of St. Lawrence County.

Most of today's homes have at least one television and many of these sets are hooked to a commercial cable system that provides a seemingly limitless number of programs. Moreover, many television programs are pushing the limits of good taste and decency. Some parents, who worry that their children are being exposed to violence and other realities of adult life that they're too young to handle, tend to say that television is the culprit, but parents need to take charge of television.

Although parents might prefer that government exert more control or networks voluntarily regulate themselves, the bottom line is that it's the parent's job to set limits on children's television viewing.

But it's not a good idea to banish the television set to a dusty attic. In fact, doing so is actually a disservice to children because the content of television shows is so deeply imbedded in the popular culture. Not knowing about Barney and Big Bird or Michael Jordan and Madonna leaves a child the odd kid out. In school, when the talk is about a certain show, those who are denied television are left with nothing to contribute.

Rather than eliminating television altogether, take a two stage approach to influencing children's viewing habits. It starts with firm limitations on both the program content and the amount of time young children are permitted to watch.

Limit Television for Preschoolers

Setting limits on television viewing is critical to your child's development. Young children are easily attracted to and seduced by the flashy colors, intense sounds and fast moving images on the television screen. While a little of this may be O.K., if a toddler is spending a good part of his day watching television, he's not doing other things that are more beneficial and even necessary to his development.

Television can be such an exciting medium for learning, but children need to use it wisely, not waste their childhood by watching things that are inappropriate or unacceptable. At this stage, there is a tremendous amount of learning to be done and most of that learning occurs when the child is playing with his toys and exploring his surroundings.

Exposure to excessive or graphic violence may make children fearful and anxious.

Preschoolers may show a preference for certain programs. Unfortunately, watching one favorite show often leads to watching television for an extended period of time. Once children start watching one show, they tend to watch other shows. This reduces the time a child has left in her day to do other things. Children who watch excessive amounts of television, spend less time involved in creative activities and vigorous exercise, and develop an unhealthy pattern of passivity.

When programs designed specifically for young children go off, the television should go off. By the time shows with adult content come on, young children should be in bed. Special seasonal programs such as "The Nutcracker" may be exceptions to this rule.

Monitor Television Use by School-Age Children

As youngsters get older, they should gradually be given more discretion over program choice, as long as parents continue to monitor their viewing habits. It's important for parents to spend time with their children in front of the set, then talk about what they've seen. Even if your children persist in choosing shows you don't wholly approve of, you'll be more effective in helping them develop discriminating taste if you go ahead and let them watch while continuing to make your opinion clear. Censoring television programs is largely ineffective with teenagers, because it makes the show exotic. Rationally evaluating the show is a more effective way to make your point.

Why Parents Should Worry

There are several other concerns about children who watch a lot of television. For some children, television is their most important teacher. If so, what are the lessons being learned? That only glamorous people populate the world? That people on television don't get hurt or die even when they are shot or are involved in accidents? That even serious problems can be solved in a half-hour? Do you want your children believing these ideas?

A recent study reports that today's preschoolers watch so much television that, by the time a child enters kindergarten, she expects the scene to change several times each minute. In order to make a classroom look like a television screen, the child constantly looks around the room to see a different scene every few seconds. This doesn't leave a lot of time to concentrate on the lesson. The next time you sit down to watch your favorite show, notice how frequently the scene changes. Is this real life?

Another concern is the amount of violence shown on television. Exposure to excessive or graphic violence may make children fearful and anxious. Some children begin to believe that violence is an acceptable way to deal with conflicts and problems. Some children are de-sensitized to violence, so that they can't feel empathy for someone who is hurt or suffering.

Children often believe everything they see and hear on television commercials. Many high priced, low nutrition snacks and cereals are advertised at times when children are watching. Candy and soft drinks are also heavily marketed on children's television programming. Children who watch a lot of television not only lack exercise, but tend to eat more and what they usually eat is junk food. The result, too often, is a child who is overweight.

During the holidays, children are bombarded with ads for expensive toys. These ads can create desires in children that put them in conflict with their parents' values.

What Can Parents Do?

What is the solution? Limit the amount of time your child watches television. Be certain the programs viewed are suitable for her age. Watch the shows and commercials with your children and talk together about what you've seen.

While parents need time for themselves, they should avoid using television to keep their children occupied while they relax and enjoy "downtime." It's better to be firm about setting reasonable bedtime hours than to let children watch any program to satisfy your own needs for peace and quiet.

Parents are so busy that they sometimes stop using plain old common sense. They may know their children shouldn't be watching a particular show, that they should be in bed but lack the energy to enforce bedtime rules. Instead of letting it go, take charge. If your kids accuse you of being too strict or too concerned, consider it the ultimate compliment. Explain that you're only doing your job, which is, after all, the most important job in the world.

Advocacy Groups Play an Important Role in Developing Media Policies for Children

Amy B. Jordan

Amy B. Jordan is director of the media and the developing child sector of the Annenberg Public Policy Center of the University of Pennsylvania.

Judgments about the success or failure of media policy to empower parents to more effectively direct children's media use or limit exposure to potentially harmful content depend, in large part, on where one stands. Evaluations of the implementation of federal mandates suggest that the media industry will follow the letter of the law. In the case of television, for example, television manufacturers began including the computer V-Chip device in television sets sold after January 2000 to comply with the Telecommunications Act of 1996. Programmers provided ratings information for television shows to comply with the V-Chip mandate. Broadcast networks listed the minimum three hours a week of educational programming for children in their FCC [Federal Communications Commission] filings under the Three-Hour Rule. But did children's exposure to the "bad" of television decrease, and did their viewing of the "good" of television increase? Research says "not really."

Federal Regulations Are Largely Ineffective

Some observers argue that media companies live up to the letter but not the spirit of the law. As a result, the usefulness of federal regulations has been widely viewed as limited in the

Amy B. Jordan, "Successes and Failure of Media Policy for Children," *Children and Electronic Media*, Vol. 18, No. 1, The Future of Children, Spring 2008. Copyright © 2008 by The Future of Children. All rights reserved. Reproduced by permission.

current media environment. A study conducted by the Annenberg Public Policy Center in the year following implementation of the V-Chip mandate found that less than 10 percent of parents consistently used the device, even when they were shown how to use it. Why? Post-experiment interviews with mothers revealed that many found the device difficult to locate (it was buried five menus into the RCA model provided) and confusing to program. Research at the Kaiser Family Foundation also suggests that the ratings are too complex to be effective for parents. A full decade after the V-Chip ratings were introduced, only 11 percent of parents know that "FV" is an indicator of violent content in children's programming.

The Three-Hour Rule has also had limited success in changing parents' practices regarding the television set. A study by the Annenberg Public Policy Center conducted two years after the mandate went into effect found that few parents knew that broadcasters were airing educational and informational programming for children. Two critical obstacles appeared to block parental awareness. First, the programs considered educational by the broadcasters (for example, *Saved by the Bell*, a comedy about high school teens) were not considered educational by parents, who held a more traditional conception of "educational." Second, parents did not recognize or understand the on-air symbol "E/I" used by broadcasters to denote educational programming.

Several years of content analyses of the commercial broadcasters' educational offerings reveal that broadcasters continue to make dubious claims about the educational value of their programs. The Annenberg Public Policy Center has consistently found that roughly one in five of the commercial broadcasters' "FCC-friendly" programs contains no discernable educational lesson. In addition, the majority of the network-provided programs are "pro-social"—they teach children lessons such as loyalty, honesty, and cooperation rather than teaching curriculum-based lessons such as science, math, or reading.

Though the Federal Communications Commission does not routinely screen programs to make judgments about whether a program is educational, it does act on complaints it receives. In 2005, the United Church of Christ raised concerns about commercial broadcast network Univision's educational programming lineup. After reviewing the complaint, the FCC fined Univision affiliates $24 million for listing rebroadcasts of steamy and violent telenovelas (such as *Complices al Rescate*) as educational programming for children.

Though 78 percent of parents say they have used movie ratings to direct children's movie viewing, only about half say they use music advisories, video game ratings, and television program ratings.

Violations of Federal Policy Are Common

Broadcast networks have also been fined for violating federal policy related to indecency. The infamous case of [singer/dancer] Janet Jackson's "wardrobe malfunction" [during the 2004 Super Bowl halftime show on CBS] raised the concern of lawmakers and catalyzed Congress to pass the Broadcast Decency Enforcement Act of 2005, which raised fines tenfold from $32,500 to $325,000 for violations. In its aftermath, FOX stations were heavily fined when [actress] Nicole Richie used profanity during the live broadcast of the Billboard Music Awards. A federal appeals court, however, found the rule "arbitrary and capricious" and ordered the FCC to reconsider its policy on "fleeting expletives." Indecency definitions, often vague, have frustrated broadcasters and social observers. [Comedian] George Carlin's famous "Seven Dirty Words" monologue highlights the challenges in legislating language, as does the inherent contradiction of punishing stations for profanity, which virtually no studies have shown to be harmful to children, but not for gratuitous violence, which dozens, possibly hundreds, of studies have shown to be problematic.

(Lawmakers and the Federal Communications Commission have recently argued that indecency definitions should include graphic violence, particularly in the wake of the blood, gore, and torture in popular programs such as FOX's *24*.)

The Federal Trade Commission [FTC], the agency charged with enforcing the Children's Online Privacy Protection Act, has also found itself in the position of fining flagrant violators of the congressional mandate. In 2006, the FTC fined the website Xanga $1 million, alleging that the site collected personal information from children whom it knew to be under thirteen years of age without having first obtained the requisite verifiable parental consent. According to the FTC, the website stated that children under thirteen were not allowed to join. But despite this disclaimer, Xanga allowed 1.7 million visitors who submitted information indicating that they were younger than thirteen to create accounts on the website. The FTC further alleged that Xanga had not provided sufficient notice on the website of how information regarding children would be used, had failed to provide direct notice to parents about the information it was collecting and how the information would be used, and had failed to allow parents access to and control over their children's information.

Violations of the industry's self-regulatory practices are less widely known, primarily because investigations are not widely publicized by the industry-funded groups that track them. Some academic research has been conducted on the voluntary ratings systems, however. In one study, researchers recruited parents to rate the content of computer and video games, movies, and television programs. Raters felt that industry labels were "too lenient" when compared with what parent coders would find suitable for children. Nor are ratings well understood. Perhaps because of ratings' inconsistencies, or perhaps because parents are not fully aware of the information offered by media, many parents do not consistently use the ratings to guide their children. Though 78 percent of parents say they have used movie ratings to direct children's movie viewing, only about half say they use music advisories, video game ratings, and television program ratings (54 percent, 52 percent, and 50 percent, respectively). Even among parents who report using industry-provided ratings and advisories, most do not find them to be "very useful," according to a Kaiser Family Foundation survey.

Advocacy Groups Have an Important Role

Advocacy groups such as Children Now, the Center for Science in the Public Interest, and the National Center for Missing and Exploited Children keep a watchful eye. The Campaign for a Commercial-Free Childhood, for example, sent a letter to the Federal Trade Commission decrying the heavy marketing of the PG-13-rated movie *Transformers* to young children through toy and food promotions. Citing CARU's [Children's Advertising Review Unit's] lack of disciplinary action, it asked the FTC to intervene. And unlike industry self-regulatory units, advocacy groups have, as part of their mission, the goal of informing the public about industry misdeeds.

The Motion Picture Production Code Is Effective in Restricting Movie Violence

Joel Timmer

Joel Timmer is an associate professor of film, television, and digital media at Texas Christian University.

Film historians examining the functioning of the Motion Picture Production Code have tended to view the Code not so much as a rigidly enforced set of rules but more as a set of guidelines open to interpretation and negotiation. Since the late 1980s, film historians have conducted several case studies using Production Code Administration (PCA) files to understand the functioning of the PCA and how it applied the Code. What has not yet been examined is how well the framers of the Code did, without much social scientific research to rely on, in identifying and restricting the types of film violence that could have negative effects on audiences. When one considers this question, one finds that the Code's drafters did amazingly well at restricting potentially harmful film violence despite the lack of relevant social scientific research at the time the Code was written.

Movies Should Uphold the Morals of Society

The Motion Picture Production Code restricted film content, particularly in the areas of sex and crime, from 1934 to 1968. Introduced and accepted by film producers in 1930, the Motion Picture Production Code was not strictly followed at that time. Upset by the ineffectiveness of the Code in restricting movie content, the Catholic Church, through its Legion of Decency, threatened a boycott of the movies in 1933. This led the industry to take new steps to ensure that films complied with the Code. The steps included requiring movie studios to submit scripts to the PCA for approval prior to filming, requiring the studios to submit finished films for approval, and fining film studios $25,000 for violating the Code. The Code remained in effect until it was replaced in 1969 with the precursor of today's Motion Picture Association of America film ratings system.

Although a major concern of the drafters of the Code, many of whom were officials within the Catholic Church, was the effects of films on their audiences, it does not appear that much research into the potential harmful effects of film content on film audiences was relied on in drafting the Code. Rather, the Code was based more on a philosophy that films should uphold the morals of society. . . .

Research Suggests Media Violence Has Negative Effects

Although there was not a great deal of research on violence effects for the Code's drafters or PCA officials to rely on in devising the Code's various provisions, much such work has been conducted in the intervening decades. Based on that research, groups such as the American Psychological Association, American Medical Association, National Academy of Science, and Centers for Disease Control and Prevention "have concluded that the mass media bear some responsibility for contributing to real world violence" [according to Barbara J. Wilson et al.]. Although research has shown that violence in films and on television may affect viewers negatively, there "is universal agreement that many factors contribute to violent behavior, such as gangs, drugs, guns, poverty, and racism"

[Wilson states]. Thus, although exposure to "media violence is not the only, nor even the most important, contributor to violent behavior" [according to Wilson], there are negative effects that may be associated with exposure to media violence.

The framers of the [Production] Code were largely successful in identifying and restricting those types of violent depictions most likely to carry the potential for harmful effects on audiences.

There are three primary negative effects that have been associated with viewing media violence. First, viewers can learn and imitate aggressive attitudes and behaviors. As a result, media violence can increase aggression in its viewers. Second, "continued exposure" to media violence can "undermine feelings of concern, empathy, or sympathy viewers might have toward victims of actual violence" [Wilson states]. This is known as a *desensitization effect*. Third, viewing media violence "can lead to fear reactions such as a general fear of crime or victimization"; in other words, viewing violence on the news and in fictional programming "may lead to the belief that the world is generally a scary and dangerous place" [according to Wilson].

Despite the potential for these harmful effects, "not all violent portrayals are equal with regard to the risk they might pose"; instead, "some depictions are more likely than others to pose risks for viewers" [Wilson states]. In other words: media violence can be presented in different ways. Some of those ways increase the likelihood of harmful effects for viewers of that violence, whereas other ways can actually decrease that likelihood. As part of the National Television Violence Study, a three-year effort to study and assess violence on television involving scholars from several universities, an effort was made to distinguish different ways violence was depicted and the effects such depictions could have on viewers. Researchers sought to "identify the contextual features associated with violent depictions that most significantly increase the risk of a harmful effect on the audience" [according to Wilson et al.]. After reviewing the scientific work done to date on the effects of television violence, the researchers were able to identify nine "contextual features that either diminish or enhance the risk of harmful effects associated with viewing violent portrayals."

Comparing these contextual features to the provisions of the Production Code dealing with depictions of violence reveals a surprising finding: the framers of the Code were largely successful in identifying and restricting those types of violent depictions most likely to carry the potential for harmful effects on audiences. . . .

The Code does correspond to a degree with what the research on contextual features shows, which is that depictions of heroes committing violent acts can have negative effects on viewers.

Nature of the Perpetrator

The first of contextual features associated with the presentation of violence is the "nature of the perpetrator." If the perpetrator, or the character committing violent acts, is "engaging or attractive," this can increase the likelihood that viewers will be negatively affected by such a violent portrayal, specifically increasing the chances that viewers "will learn aggression" from that portrayal. This is because an attractive or engaging perpetrator can act as a "potent role model, particularly for children." . . .

The characteristic of the perpetrator that the Code addresses most directly is the perpetrator who is the hero: "The Code specifically states that 'Criminals should not be made heroes, even if they are historical criminals'" [according to

Olga J. Martin]. This does not mean that anyone who commits a crime cannot be the hero of a film under the Code. Rather, "It is the habitual criminal rather than the first offender who comes under this classification." Accordingly, the Code specifically bans certain types of characters from being heroes in films:

> The Code ... definitely bans certain types of criminals for presentation on the screen as heroes. Thus a gangster cannot be made a hero; nor can a racketeer who is the prototype of the gangster; the kidnapper; the hardened and unregenerate type of criminal; or the type of character who seeks to fight crime by using criminal methods and so romanticizes crime and makes it appear heroic and praiseworthy.

Thus, the Code does correspond to a degree with what the research on contextual features shows, which is that depictions of heroes committing violent acts can have negative effects on viewers. The Code did forbid the portrayal of a hero of a film as a criminal, specifically listing some types of criminals, many of whom would be likely to commit violent acts, as characters who could not be heroes. . . .

Nature of the Target

The characteristics of the target of violent acts can also influence whether the depiction of those acts is more likely to lead to negative effects for viewers. Unlike most of the other contextual features, the nature of the target is less likely to cause viewers to learn aggression. Rather, it is more likely "to influence audience fear" [according to Wilson et al.]. The characteristics of the target more likely to increase audience fear are similar to those of the nature of the perpetrator more likely to lead viewers to learn violent or aggressive behaviors: being perceived as attractive by audiences, acting benevolently or heroically, being perceived as similar to the viewer, and sharing viewers' emotional experiences. The reason these victim characteristics can cause audience fear is that a "well-liked character can encourage audience involvement" and when "such a character is threatened or attacked in a violent scene, viewers are likely to experience increased anxiety and fear" [Wilson states].

There are only a couple of Code provisions dealing with the identity or characteristics of the victims of film violence. Under the Code, "no police officers, bank guards, private detectives, or other private or public servants of the law can be shown actually dying at the hands of criminals" [according to Martin]. This is consistent with the research to a degree, as law enforcement officials may be more likely to be perceived as acting "benevolently or heroically." However, the Code only prohibited such characters from being murdered by criminals. It did not prohibit their being the victims of nonlethal violence. Another Code provision prohibited films from depicting kidnappings when the person kidnapped was a child. Other than the possibility that the audience may like or feel involved with a child character, this Code provision does not directly match up with the research. . . .

If violence is depicted as humorous, this can increase the likelihood of viewers learning aggression as well as desensitizing viewers to the seriousness of violent behaviors.

Presence of Weapons

If weapons are present in a violent portrayal, particularly if the weapons are "conventional ones like guns and knives," this can increase the risk that viewers will behave aggressively [states Wilson et al.]. It has been suggested that weapons can act as visual cues that can "activate or 'prime' aggressive thoughts and behaviors in viewers" [states Wilson]. Conventional weapons, such as guns or knives, are more likely to activate aggressive thoughts or behaviors "because they are commonly associated with previous violent events stored in memory" [Wilson says].

The Code states, "There must be no display, at any time, of machine guns, sub-machine guns, or other weapons generally classified as illegal, in the hands of gangsters or other criminals." Also, "[g]uns should not be shown unless absolutely essential to the plot, and even then their use must be definitely restricted." Further, "[e]xcessive gunplay and flaunting of guns are also prohibited" and the "flaunting of weapons by gangsters, or other criminals, will not be allowed".

The Code, then, does restrict the depiction of guns. Guns could not be shown at all unless essential to the plot. Further, specific types of guns, such as machine guns or other illegal weapons, could not be depicted in the hands of gangsters or criminals. . . .

Humor

If violence is depicted as humorous, this can increase the likelihood of viewers learning aggression as well as desensitizing viewers to the seriousness of violent behaviors. Although there is limited research in this area, there is some evidence to indicate that "humor combined with violence actually can foster aggression"; one possible explanation for this is that "humor may diminish the seriousness of the violence and therefore undermine the inhibiting effects of harm and pain cues in a scene" [according to Wilson et al.]. . . .

For its part, only one provision of the Code seems to deal with humor being coupled with violent acts. Under the Code, rape "should never be treated as comedy." . . .

Motive for the Violence

Another contextual feature deals with the "motive or reason for the violence" [cited Wilson]. If the violence appears to be "justified or morally defensible," this can increase the likelihood of negative effects, particularly the learning of aggression, from such a portrayal. More specifically, viewing violence that is motivated by the protection of one's self or another, or that is an act of retaliation for a past wrong, can increase viewer aggression. On the other hand, unjustified violence can decrease the risk that one will learn aggression from the portrayal. If the violence is "purely malicious" or otherwise unjustified, viewers are less likely to imitate the behavior or learn aggression. . . .

The Code was quite clear that wrongdoing could not be rewarded in films, nor could it go unpunished.

The Code is clear in specifying that criminal acts, killing, and murder may not be made to appear justified in films. For example:

> If the hero or sympathetic character in a story is shown to commit murder as a means of retribution or to serve some other apparently justifiable end, the audience is likely to forget that murder, per se, is wrong, and to feel that it may be right some times. Such a reaction is definitely dangerous and anti-social, and for this reason any story which seeks to justify a murder is automatically disqualified for screen presentation. . . .

Reward or Punishment

The likelihood of viewers learning aggression can be increased when violent behavior is rewarded or goes unpunished. Unpunished violent acts can also increase a viewer's fear, particularly if the violence seems to be random or unjust. Although it has been shown that viewers of scenes containing aggressive behavior that is rewarded are more likely to act aggressively than those of scenes where aggressive behavior is punished, it is not necessary for aggressive behavior in a scene to be explicitly rewarded for it to have a negative effect on viewers. As long as the aggressive behavior in a scene is not explicitly punished, it can still increase the likelihood of a viewer acting aggressively, much as it would if the aggressive behavior were rewarded. In other words, if violent behavior is not clearly punished in some way, there is an increased risk of aggressive behavior by viewers. On the other hand, it has been shown that observing scenes in which perpetrators are punished for their violent acts can decrease viewer aggression and viewer fear.

As the PCA stated regarding its interpretation of its crime regulations: "The intent of the Code is . . . to insure above all that crime will be shown to be *wrong*, and that the criminal life will be loathed, and that the law will *at all times prevail*". Thus, characters who committed violent criminal acts in films could not be rewarded but in fact needed to be punished in some manner, or at the very least, it needed to be made clear to the audience in some other way that the commission of such an act was definitely wrong. Further, the Code states, "Even though punished, the 'sin' or crime must not be made so attractive that in the end the condemnation will be forgotten and only the apparent joy of the sin will be remembered." . . .

On this point, then, the Code and the contextual effects research are in accordance. As the research shows, not only do violent acts that are rewarded carry the risk of negative effects in viewers but so do such acts that go unpunished. The Code was quite clear that wrongdoing could not be rewarded in films, nor could it go unpunished. Instead, it was necessary that the perpetrators of violent criminal acts be punished in some way, and that it be made clear to the audience that such acts were wrong.

Extent or Graphicness of Violence

If the violence portrayed is extensive or graphic, then the likelihood of negative effects in viewers can be greater. Exposure to extensive, graphic violence can increase the likelihood of viewers behaving aggressively, of viewers becoming desensitized to violence, and of viewers' feeling increased levels of fear. For example, there is evidence to suggest that exposure to extensive media violence promotes a viewer's learning of aggression, and this effect is predicted by a number of theories as well. Also, being exposed to extensive violence, whether in a single program or film or across several programs or films, has been shown to produce a desensitization effect in viewers. With desensitization, viewers become less physiologically aroused and less sensitive to violence after exposure to extensive violence. It has also been shown that exposure to extensive violence can increase viewers' feelings of fear.

The Code states, "Excessive horror and gruesomeness will not be permitted." As Martin explains in *Hollywood's Movie Commandments*:

> If it were not for this simple little sentence in the Code the movie audiences would be exposed to such visual details in the films as disfigured, dismembered, bloodstained and mutilated bodies, close-up views of dying men, and hair-raising details of inhuman treatment. The Code, however, under this provision bans such details from the screen, permitting their introduction into a picture only by way of indirect suggestion.

Only when "it is necessary to the plot of the story to indicate brutality" may it "be suggested in such a way that the audience is not subjected to its horror-provoking details." . . .

There also seems to be some recognition in the Code that exposure to violence can lead to desensitization in audience members. As explained in the Code, "'action showing the taking of human life, even in the mystery stories, is to be cut to the minimum' because 'these frequent presentations of murder tend to lessen regard for the sacredness of life.'" Again, this statement was included in the Code despite the lack of contemporary scientific research to support it. Research done since then shows that exposure to graphic and extensive violence may cause negative effects in viewers, including desensitization. The Code, then, in being quite clear that graphic or extensive violence could not be depicted in films, was written in such away as to reduce the potential for negative effects in audience members from exposure to such violence.

Realism

If the violence portrayed seems realistic, this can increase the likelihood of viewers learning aggressive attitudes and behaviors as well as increase viewers' fear. A number of studies have shown that "realistic portrayals of violence can pose more risks for viewers than unrealistic ones" [Wilson states]. It has been suggested that when violence is depicted realistically, viewers may identify with the perpetrators more easily and that, because of the depiction's similarity to real-life situations, their inhibitions against aggressive behavior may also be reduced. In addition, viewers are more likely to experience fear after being exposed to a realistic depiction of violence as opposed to one that is not realistic.

While some depictions of consequences to the victim that might have reduced the likelihood of negative effects in viewers would not be allowed under the Code, the Code otherwise allowed the depiction of negative consequences for victims of violence.

Many of the Code provisions discussed in the previous section on the Code and explicit and graphic depictions of violence would seem to apply to realistic portrayals of violence, in that showing the details of violent acts would seem, in many cases, to make the portrayals of that violence more realistic. Apart from those provisions, however, the Code does not directly address realism in the depiction of violence in films. . . .

Consequences to the Victim

Finally, when the physical harm and pain that a victim of violence suffers as the result of a violent act is explicitly depicted, viewer learning of aggression can be decreased or inhibited. Viewers of violent scenes in which the victim of violence shows some sign of pain and suffering have been shown to act less aggressively after viewing such a scene compared to viewers of scenes of violence where no pain or suffering is shown. In other words, "for most viewers the explicit depiction of psychological and physical harm in violent portrayals is likely to inhibit the learning of aggressive attitudes and behaviors" [according to Wilson et al.].

On the whole, the drafters of the Code were largely and surprisingly effective in devising restrictions that prohibited or restricted the types of violent portrayals that research decades later would show carried the greatest risks of negative effects for viewers.

This is one area where the restrictions of the Code require violence to be portrayed in a way that is more likely to have negative effects on viewers. As discussed above, the Code generally prohibited explicit or graphic depictions of violence, including those of the injuries suffered by victims of violent acts. Although films could not graphically or explicitly depict the injuries suffered by victims of violence under the Code, the Code did not restrict—nor require—the depiction of harm or pain and suffering by victims so long as it was not graphic. So, while some depictions of consequences to the victim that might have reduced the likelihood of negative effects in viewers would not be allowed under the Code, the Code otherwise allowed the depiction of negative consequences for victims of violence.

The Drafters Did Amazingly Well

The drafters of the Code did not rely on scientific research regarding the negative effects film violence may have on audiences. Nonetheless, they did amazingly well in creating Code provisions restricting film violence that largely restricted the depiction of the types of film violence that would have the greatest likelihood of negatively affecting audience members. The Code prevented criminals from being the hero of a film. The Code placed some restrictions on the depiction of guns. The Code prohibited violent crimes from being portrayed as justified. The Code did not allow violent crimes to be rewarded or even to go unpunished but explicitly required some form of negative consequences for the perpetrators of violent crimes. And, the Code did not allow violence to be portrayed in a graphic or explicit manner. In all of these ways, the Code placed restrictions on those contextual features shown by research to carry the greatest risk of negative effects.

Many of these Code provisions are an outgrowth of the Code's focus on films "proving the thesis that crime does not pay; that it is wrong, and that it brings suffering and punishment to the offender." Along these lines, the Code sought to ensure that films would not "be construed as to leave the question of right or wrong in doubt or fogged," "throw the sympathy of the audience with . . . crime, wrong-doing, or evil," or "present evil alluringly." These objectives led to restrictions that are consistent with the contextual features more likely to have negative effects dealing with the nature of perpetrator, motive for violence, and reward or punishment. In other areas, the drafters, of the Code seemed to want to protect audiences from being exposed to scenes that were too explicit or graphic. These provisions led to restrictions consistent with the research on the potentially harmful contextual features of the presence of weapons, the extent or graphicness of violence, and realism.

The drafters of the Code did allow some depictions of violence in films that are associated with the risk of negative effects for audience members. The Code allowed violence to be perpetrated by characters who might be attractive and engaging to the audience. It had little to say on the characteristics of the victims of violent behavior. It allowed depictions of knives in violent scenes, and it did not allow explicit or graphic depictions of injuries to the victims of violence. Nevertheless, on the whole, the drafters of the Code were largely and surprisingly effective in devising restrictions that prohibited or restricted the types of violent portrayals that research decades later would show carried the greatest risks of negative effects for viewers. In this regard, the Code's drafters were, by and large, successful in crafting restrictions to achieve their objective that "[n]o picture should lower the moral standards of those who see it."

Movie Ratings
Are an Ineffective Form
of Censorship

Nicholas Ransbottom

Nicholas Ransbottom is a staff writer for The Charleston Gazette.

A s a writer and advocate of freedom of expression, censorship is one of my hot-button issues. I find it appalling that some people think it's a good idea to keep others from experiencing something the way it was meant to be experienced. Perhaps this is why I find the ratings given to films by the Motion Picture Association of America [MPAA] to be utterly useless.

Movie Ratings Are Arbitrary

What started as an attempt to guide parents on whether or not a film was appropriate for children has turned into a process to bastardize the artistic nature of film by giving it a rating.

For instance, the film "Boys Don't Cry" featured sexually explicit scenes that were intended to be brutal and unglamorous, but it was forced to be cut in order not to get an NC-17 rating, which, for distributors, is a death sentence. The film "A Clockwork Orange" featured unadulterated violence and sexual activity and was slapped with an X rating. (NC-17 replaced the X rating in 1990).

What's troublesome about this is that the MPAA seems to let films off the hook depending on how they handle violence. It plays favorites.

For example, [director] Steven Spielberg's World War II film "Saving Private Ryan" is much more disturbing than the satirical "Clockwork," but the violence in it was filmed more artistically, using lots of slow motion and dramatic music. Because of the way the violence is handled, the film's rating was toned down.

And that's the problem with not only the MPAA ratings system but censorship as a whole. People have different tastes, find different things offensive and are disturbed by different things. No group of people has a right to tell another group of people what they are and are not allowed to experience.

Temptation is a basic human emotion, and when you tell people they aren't allowed to do something, they're going to want to do it more than ever.

There's a fantastic scene in "Inside Deep Throat," a documentary about the pornographic film "Deep Throat," that shows an interview with a woman in her late 60s at the release of the movie. "I wanted to see a dirty picture and I saw a dirty picture," she says.

That's the kicker with these movie ratings: they don't work. They don't stop people from seeing a movie.

Theaters don't even enforce them. I've been seeing R-rated movies in a theater by myself since I was 12. The only thing the amount of violence, sex and drug use that I've been exposed to has done to me is make me realize how hypocritical the ratings system is.

Temptation is a basic human emotion, and when you tell people they aren't allowed to do something, they're going to want to do it more than ever. This is the basis for many mythological tales, such as Adam and Eve and Pandora's Box.

I wouldn't have much of a problem if these ratings were simply guidelines, but when they lead to people being denied access to art, it bothers me—especially because, in the end, their attempt at denial fails.

Organizations to Contact

The editors have compiled the following list of organizations concerned with the issues debated in this book. The descriptions are derived from materials provided by the organizations. All have publications or information available for interested readers. The list was compiled on the date of publication of the present volume; names, addresses, phone and fax numbers, and e-mail and Internet addresses may change. Be aware that many organizations take several weeks or longer to respond to inquiries, so allow as much time as possible.

American Civil Liberties Union (ACLU)
125 Broad St., 18th Floor, New York, NY   10004
(212) 549-2500 • fax: (212) 869-9065
e-mail: infoaclu@aclu.org
website: www.aclu.org

The American Civil Liberties Union is a national organization that works to defend Americans' civil rights as guaranteed in the US Constitution. The ACLU works in courts, legislatures, and communities to defend First Amendment rights, the right to equal protection, the right to due process, and the right to privacy. The ACLU publishes the semiannual newsletter *Civil Liberties Alert* in addition to policy statements and reports.

Center for Media Literacy (CML)
22631 Pacific Coast Hwy., Suite 472, Malibu, CA   90265
(310) 804-3985 • fax: (310) 456-0020
e-mail: cml@medialit.org
website: www.medialit.org

The Center for Media Literacy is an educational organization that works to help children and adults prepare for living and learning in a global media culture. CML works to achieve this goal by translating media literacy research and theory into training and educational tools for teachers, youth leaders, parents, and caregivers of children. CML publishes a newsletter, studies, reports, and curriculum materials, including the teaching resource "Beyond Blame: Challenging Violence in the Media."

Entertainment Software Rating Board (ESRB)

317 Madison Ave., 22nd Floor, New York, NY   10017

(212) 759-0700

website: www.esrb.org

The Entertainment Software Rating Board is a nonprofit, self-regulatory body established in 1994 by the Entertainment Software Association (ESA) to empower consumers, especially parents, with the ability to make informed decisions about the computer and video games they choose for their families. ESRB assigns computer and video game content ratings, enforces industry-adopted advertising guidelines, and helps ensure responsible online privacy practices for the interactive entertainment software industry. ESRB publishes many resources aimed at parents with information about video games, including "A Parent's Guide to Video Games: Parental Controls and Online Safety."

Federal Communications Commission (FCC)

445 12th St. SW, Washington, DC   20554

(888) 225-5322 • fax: (866) 418-0232

e-mail: fccinfo@fcc.gov

website: www.fcc.gov

The Federal Communications Commission is an independent US government agency charged with regulating interstate and international communications by radio, television, wire, satellite, and cable. The FCC's Enforcement Bureau enforces federal law that prohibits obscene programming and limits indecent or profane programming. The FCC's website contains information about television ratings and has information about how to file a complaint.

First Amendment Center

1207 18th Ave. S, Nashville, TN   37212
(615) 727-1600 • fax: (615) 727-1319
website: www.firstamendmentcenter.org

The First Amendment Center works to preserve and protect First Amendment freedoms through information and education. The center serves as a forum for the study and exploration of free-expression issues, including freedom of speech, freedom of the press, religious liberty, freedom of assembly, and freedom to petition the government. It has a wide variety of publications available on its website, including the overview, "Violence and the Media."

Free Expression Policy Project (FEPP)

e-mail: margeheins@verizon.net
website: www.fepproject.org

The Free Expression Policy Project is a think tank that focuses on upholding artistic and intellectual freedom. FEPP provides research and advocacy on free speech, copyright, and media democracy issues. Available at FEPP's website are numerous commentaries on issues of free expression, including "Requiem for California's Violent Video Games Law."

Freedom Forum

555 Pennsylvania Ave. NW, Washington, DC   20001
(202) 292-6353
e-mail: news@freedomforum.org
website: www.freedomforum.org

The Freedom Forum is a nonpartisan foundation dedicated to free press, free speech, and free spirit for all people. The Freedom Forum's First Amendment Center works to preserve and protect First Amendment freedoms through information and education. It publishes the annual report, "State of the First Amendment."

International Clearinghouse on Children, Youth and Media
NORDICOM, University of Gothenburg, Box 713
Göteborg   SE 405 30
   Sweden
(46) 31-786-1000 • fax: (46) 31-786-4658
e-mail: clearinghouse@nordicom.gu.se
website: www.nordicom.gu.se/clearinghouse.php

The aim of the International Clearinghouse on Children, Youth and Media is to increase awareness and knowledge about children, youth, and media. It seeks to provide a basis for relevant policymaking, contribute to the public debate, and enhance children's and young people's media literacy. The Clearinghouse informs various groups of users—researchers, policymakers, media professionals, voluntary organizations, teachers, students, and interested individuals. Books on media violence can be purchased on its website.

Media Coalition
19 Fulton St., Suite 407, New York, NY   10038
(212) 587-4025 • fax: (212) 587-2436
website: www.mediacoalition.org

Media Coalition is an association that defends the First Amendment right to produce and sell books, movies, magazines, recordings, DVDs, videotapes, and video games. Media Coalition represents professional media groups by engaging in legal advocacy, congressional research, and legislative action in support of free expression. Available at its website are the amicus briefs filed in support of the First Amendment and news on recent First Amendment legislation.

Morality in Media (MIM)
1100 G St. NW, Suite 1030, Washington, DC   20005
(202) 393-7245 • fax: (202) 393-1717
e-mail: mim@moralityinmedia.org
website: www.moralityinmedia.org

Morality in Media (MIM) is a national nonprofit organization established to combat obscenity and uphold decency standards in the media. MIM works to inform the public about the harms of indecent media and works to maintain standards of decency on television and in other media. MIM publishes a quarterly newsletter, *Morality in Media Newsletter,* as well as several articles, including "What the Public Thinks About Sex, Vulgarity, and Violence on Television."

National Center for Children Exposed to Violence (NCCEV)
230 S Frontage Rd., New Haven, CT   06520-7900
(877) 496-2238 • fax: (203) 785-4608
e-mail: colleen.vadala@yale.edu
website: www.nccev.org

The National Center for Children Exposed to Violence works to increase the capacity of individuals and communities to reduce the incidence and impact of violence on children and families. It trains and supports the professionals who provide intervention and treatment to children and families affected, and seeks to increase public awareness of the effects of violence—including media violence—on children, families, communities, and society. The center's website has a section on media violence including information on relevant websites, statistics, and a list of recommended reports, books, and articles.

Parents Television Council (PTC)
707 Wilshire Blvd., Suite 2075, Los Angeles, CA   90017
(800) 882-6868 • fax: (213) 403-1301
e-mail: editor@parentstv.org
website: www.parentstv.org

The Parents Television Council is an advocacy organization whose primary mission is to promote and restore responsibility and decency to the entertainment industry. The PTC seeks to discourage the graphic sexual themes, depictions of gratuitous violence, and profane language in broadcast television through citizen action. Among the PTC's special reports are "Top 10 Best and Worst Advertisers" and "The Alarming Family Hour . . . No Place for Children."

Teachers Resisting Unhealthy
Children's Entertainment (TRUCE)
160 Lakeview Ave., Cambridge, MA   02138
e-mail: truce@truceteachers.org
website: www.truceteachers.org

Teachers Resisting Unhealthy Children's Entertainment is a national group of educators concerned about how children's entertainment is affecting the play and behavior of children in classrooms nationwide. Its goals are to raise public awareness about the negative effects of violent and stereotyped media and to support parents' and teachers' efforts to deal with the issues regarding media. TRUCE offers guides and resources online.

Bibliography

Books

Tom Bissell

Extra Lives: Why Video Games Matter. New York: Pantheon Books, 2010.

James Paul Gee

What Video Games Have to Teach Us About Learning and Literacy, 2nd ed. New York: Palgrave Macmillan, 2007.

Mary Heston

Violent Games—Violent Children. Las Vegas, NV: Internet Medical Association, 2011.

Gerard Jones

Killing Monsters: Why Children Need Fantasy, Super Heroes, and Make-Believe Violence. New York: Basic Books, 2002.

Steven J. Kirsh

Children, Adolescents, and Media Violence: A Critical Look at the Research. Los Angeles, CA: Sage Publications, 2012.

Lawrence Kutner and Cheryl Olson

Grand Theft Childhood: The Surprising Truth About Violent Video Games and What Parents Can Do. New York: Simon & Schuster, 2008.

Jane McGonigal

Reality Is Broken: Why Games Make Us Better and How They Can Change the World. New York: Penguin Press, 2011.

Tom Pollard   *Sex and Violence: The Hollywood Censorship Wars.* Boulder, CO: Paradigm Publishers, 2009.

Scott Rigby and Richard Ryan   *Glued to Games: How Video Games Draw Us In and Hold Us Spellbound.* Santa Barbara, CA: ABC-CLIO, 2011.

Tricia Rose   *The Hip Hop Wars: What We Talk About When We Talk About Hip Hop—And Why It Matters.* New York: Basic Books, 2008.

Jody Santos   *Daring to Feel: Violence, the News Media, and Their Emotions.* Lanham, MD: Lexington Books, 2009.

Laura J. Shepherd   *Gender, Violence and Popular Culture: Telling Stories.* New York: Routledge, 2013.

Scott Steinberg   *The Modern Parent's Guide to Kids and Video Games.* Lilburn, GA: Power Play Publishing, 2011.

David Trend   *The Myth of Media Violence: A Critical Introduction.* Malden, MA: Blackwell Publishing, 2007.

Erika Wittekind   *Violence as Entertainment: Why Aggression Sells.* North Mankato, MN: Compass Point Books, 2012.

Periodicals and Internet Sources

Jane Anderson   "Violent Media Desensitizes Boys to Aggression," *Pediatric News*, vol. 44, no. 11, November 2010.

Gary Giumetti and Patrick Markey	"Violent Video Games and Anger as Predictors of Aggression," *Journal of Research in Personality*, 2007.
Marjorie Heins	"Of Liberals and Conservatives: Using 'Common Sense' to Censor Video Games," Free Expression Policy Project, November 4, 2010. www.fepproject.org/index.html.
Denise Herd	"Changing Images of Violence in Rap Music Lyrics: 1979–1997," *Journal of Public Health Policy*, vol. 30, no. 4, 2009.
Randye Hoder	"Remixing Parental Objections into Rap Lyrics," *New York Times*, August 19, 2012.
Josh Kraushaar	"Stop the Blame Game," *National Journal*, January 11, 2011. www.nationaljournal.com.
Helen Lewis-Hasteley	"Violent Video Games Might Be Tasteless, but Are They Dangerous?" *New Statesman*, August 8, 2011. www.newstatesman.com.
Stephen Marche	"Are Things Getting a Little Violent? A Thousand Words About Our Culture," *Esquire*, August 2008. www.esquire.com.
Stephen Marche	"Don't Blame the Movie, but Don't Ignore It Either," *New York Times*, July 26, 2012.

Patrick McCormick	"Moral Kombat: How Much Should We Worry About the Daily Dose of Interactive, Virtual Murder and Mayhem in Our Kids' Lives?" *U.S. Catholic*, April 2009. www.uscatholic.org.
Zarina Patel	"Computer/Video Games—Two Sides of a Coin," *Business Recorder*, December 10, 2011.
B.A. Primack et al.	"Role of Video Games in Improving Health-Related Outcomes: A Systematic Review," *American Journal of Preventative Medicine*, vol. 42, no. 6, June 2012.
ScienceDaily	"Violent Video Games Alter Brain Function in Young Men," December 1, 2011. www.sciencedaily.com.
ScienceDaily	"Violent Video Games Reduce Brain Response to Violence and Increase Aggressive Behavior, Study Suggests," May 26, 2011. www.sciencedaily.com.
Suchitra Sharma	"TV and Computers Contribute to Juvenile Delinquency: Psychiatrists Say Such Behaviour Stems from Watching Violent Content on TV," *Daily News & Analysis*, April 13, 2012.
Aisha Sultan	"Violent Video Games Not a Safe Outlet for Aggression, Doctor Says," *St. Louis Post-Dispatch*, March 28, 2009.

Jim Taylor	"Parenting: Take the Offensive Against Popular Culture," *Psychology Today*, October 14, 2010.
E. Vlasak and M. Ranaldo	"Video Games," *The Exceptional Parent*, vol. 42, 2012.
S. David Wilson	"Don't Blame Video Games for Violence," *Hamilton Spectator*, March 20, 2009.

Index

A

A rating for movies, 48
Academic achievement and rap music, 38–39
Ad Meter, 81
AdBowl, 81
Advertising violence and humor
  changes in, 80
  implications of, 81–82
  increases in, 75–82
  interface, 77–79
  likeability in, 80–81
  overview, 75
  studies on, 75–77
  during Super Bowl, 79–80
Advocacy groups
  federal policy violations, 141–143
  federal regulations and, 139–141
  overview, 139
  role in media policies, 139–143
  role of, 143
African Americans, 26, 28, 29
Aggression/aggressive behavior
  baby rage, 92–94
  measuring in lab, 101–102
  media violence and, 83–88
  overview, 83–84
  reward or punishment and, 151–152
  from television violence, 70–74, 84–86
  video game violence, 84, 86–88
Alcohol abuse, 32, 38, 89–91

American Academy of Child and Adolescent Psychiatry, 31, 83, 131
American Academy of Family Physicians, 83
American Academy of Pediatrics (AAP), 72, 83, 131
American Civil Liberties Union, 132
American Medical Association, 83, 145
American Psychiatric Association, 83
American Psychological Association, 17, 83, 145
Anderson, Craig A., 17, 83–88
Anderson, James A., 95–99
Animated film violence, 73
Annenberg Public Policy Center, 140
Annual Review of Public Health, 111
Anterior cingulate cortex, 127
Anti-communist newspapers, 55
Aristotle (Greek philosopher), 16
Armstrong, Eric, 30–31
Asbridge, Mark, 21–29
Asian Americans, 26, 27–29

B

Baby rage, 92–94
Bandura, Albert, 75
Bavelier, Daphne, 106
The Beatles, 17
Benedek, Laslo, 49, 50, 53

Bergen, Lori, 95–99
Berman, Pandro, 56, 61
Billboard (magazine), 21
Billboard Music Awards, 141
BioShock (video game), 122–123, 125
Bjorkqvist, Kaj, 85
The Blackboard Jungle (Hunter), 46, 56–65
Black Entertainment Television (BET), 33, 43
Blackford, Benjamin J., 75–82
Boettcher, W.A., III, 37
Boyse, Kyla, 70–74
Breen, Joseph, 47, 49, 55
Breivik, Anders Behring, 110
Bristol University, 108
British Board of Film Censors (BBFC), 47–49, 53
Broadcast Decency Enforcement Act, 141
Brooks, Richard, 56–57, 61
Brown, Chris, 33, 44
Brown v. Board of Education, 62
Bryson, Bethany, 25
Burton, Nsenga K., 18

C

Call of Duty (video game), 110
Carlin, George, 141
Catholic Church, 145
Censors/censorship
    arguments for, 16
    export censorship, 65
    of films, 51, 62
    of media violence, 16, 97, 100
    movie ratings as, 158–159
    pre-export censorship, 55
    self-regulatory, 46
    of television, 136
Center for Media Literacy, 132
Center for Science in the Public Interest, 143
Center For Successful Parenting, 127–129
Centers for Disease Control and Prevention (CDC), 111, 145
Chandler, Raymond, 124
Children Now, 143
Children's Advertising Review Unit (CARU), 143
Children's Online Privacy Protection Act, 142
Claes, M., 38
Coates, Delman, 34–35
Cobb, M.D., 37
Cognitive Daily website, 131
Cold War, 55
Columbine High School shooting, 17–18, 30
Commercial-Free Childhood, 143
Common Sense Media, 131
Copley, Jennifer, 36–41
Criminal behavior and rap music, 27–29
Crowther, Bosley, 53, 58

D

Daily Mail (newspaper), 127
Dartmouth Medical School, 89–90
Death Race (arcade game), 17
Defender (video game), 120
Delinquent behavior and rap music, 38
Depression, 32, 39, 111
Desensitization effect
    defined, 146

graphic violence and, 152–153
humor and, 76, 77, 79, 150
media violence and, 72, 78–79, 117–118
Doom (video game), 18, 123
Drug abuse, 32, 38
Duke Nukem (video game), 123
Duncan, Nikita, 109–112

E

Eminem (rapper), 31
Empathy feelings, 72, 107, 137, 146
Enough Is Enough Campaign, 33, 34, 42
Entertainment Software Ratings Board, 86
Escobar-Chaves, Soledad Liliana, 83–88
Experimenter demand effect, 102

F

Facial anger, 87
Family structure influences, 26
Fear from television violence, 74
Fear-mongering effect, 98
Federal Communications Commission (FCC), 139–141
Federal policy violations, 141–143
Federal regulations of media, 139–141
Federal Trade Commission (FTC), 83, 142, 143
Federal video game regulations, 17
Film violence. *See* Movie violence
First Amendment, 100, 132
Flare (magazine), 116–118
Ford, Glenn, 57

Foreign Relations Committee, 64
FOX stations, 141
Francis, Anne, 58
Free Expression Policy Project, 100–104
Freedman, Jonathan, 101
French rap, 38
Functional magnetic resonance imaging scans (fMRIs), 126–127

G

Game addiction, 107–108
Gangsta rap music, 30–31, 38
Gears of War (video game), 120
Gentile, Douglas A., 106
Grand Theft Auto (video game), 124
Graphic violence, 32, 152–154
Green, C. Shawn, 106
Grimes, Tom, 95–99
Grossman, David, 118

H

Haley, Bill, 61
Han, Doug Hyun, 106–107
Harris, Eric, 17–18
Hayes, Margaret, 58
Hebdige, Dick, 24
Henson, Melissa, 34, 43
Hinckley, John, 17
Hip-hop music
  artists of, 21
  preference for, 25, 39
  violence concerns with, 30
Hodenfield, Milton, 50
Holmes, James, 18
Homicide rates, 127–128
Hoodlumism, 49–50, 52, 54, 58

Hooliganism, 53, 54
Howard-Jones, Paul, 108
Humor and violence, 150
Hunter, Evan, 56

I

Indiana University School of
  Medicine, 113
Industry Ears, 33, 34, 42

J

Jackson, Janet, 141
Jenkins, Bill, 106–108
Johnson, J., 36
Jordan, Amy B., 139–143
Journal of Children and Media, 34
Judas Priest (rock band), 22
Juvenile delinquency, 48–49

K

Kaiser Family Foundation, 131,
  140, 143
Kaufman, Gil, 42–44
Keenan, Kate, 94
Kefauver, Estes, 48–49, 63–64
Kiley, Richard, 58
Killing urges in children, 116–118
King, Cynthia M., 76
Klebold, Dylan, 17–18
Knorr, Caroline, 131
Koop, C. Everett, 119
Kramer, Stanley, 49–51

L

L.A. Noire (video game), 124
Laing, David, 24
Lane, Anthony, 18

Lee, Debra, 34
Lee, Seungseob, 110
Legion of Decency, 145
Ley, Larry, 128
Lileks, James, 122–125
Lipton, Michael, 114–115
Luban, Milton, 53
Luce, Claire Booth, 64
Lyle, Jack, 16
Lyrics and violence. *See* Music
  lyrics and video violence

M

Maher, Timothy, 119–121
Manson, Charles, 17
Manson, Marilyn, 30
Martin, Olga J., 148, 153
Matthews, Vincent P., 128–129
Media education, 132–133
Media technology, 71–72
Media violence
  causes aggression, 83–88
  censoring of, 96
  does not cause aggression,
    100–104
  foundational principles of,
    96–99
  graphic violence, 32, 152–154
  introduction, 16–19
  negative effects of, 145–147
  no negative effects of, 95–99,
    101–102
  nonviolent people and, 102–
    103
  overview, 95–96, 100
  risk factors in, 88
  societal response to, 130–133,
    131–133

See also Advertising violence and humor; Movie violence; Music lyrics and video violence; Television violence; Video game violence

Meinel, Carolyn, 119–121

Mental illness, 97

Merzenich, Michael M., 106–108

Milner, Peter, 110

Miranda, D., 38

Misogynist lyrics, 30–31

Misogyny and rap music, 37–38

Mooring, William, 64

Morality of movies, 144–145

Morrow, Vic, 57

Mortal Kombat (video game), 17, 120

Motion Picture Association of America (MPAA), 57, 158

Motion Picture Production Code
drafters of, 156–157
effectiveness of, 144–157
graphic violence, 152–154
humor and, 150
media violence and, 145–147
morality and, 144–145
nature of the perpetrator, 147–148
nature of the target, 148–149
overview, 144
realistic violence, 154
reward or punishment, 151–152
victim consequences, 155
violence motive, 150–151
weapons, presence in films, 149–150

Movie ratings, 48, 90–91, 143, 158–159

Movie violence
alcohol abuse and, 89–91
as cause of criminality, 16, 18
censoring of, 46–69
classroom crime, 56–65
overview, 46–49, 89–90
R-rated movies, 90–91
street crime, 49–56

Mr. Rogers' Neighborhood (TV show), 101

Munger, Dave, 131

Murray, John P., 76

Music lyrics and video violence
mirrors societal violence, 42–44
overview, 17, 21–29, 42
teen risk of, 32
violence link, 30–32
wrong message from, 33–35
See also Hip-hop music; Rap music

N

National Academy of Science, 145

National Center for Missing and Exploited Children, 143

National Education Association, 63

National Institute of Mental Health, 83

National Institute on Alcohol Abuse and Alcoholism, 89

National Television Violence Study, 146

Nature of the perpetrator, 147–148

Nature of the target, 148–149

Nature Reviews Neuroscience (magazine), 106

New Yorker (magazine), 18

New York Times (newspaper), 53
Night Trap (video game), 17

O

Olds, James, 110

P

Pac-Man (video game), 119–121, 124
Parental influence
    media monitoring by, 134–138
    overview, 134–135
    television concerns, 136–138
    television limits, 135–136
    Three-Hour Rule, 139, 140
Parents Television Council (PTC), 33–35, 34, 42–43
Parker, Edwin B., 16
Paxton, John, 49–50
Payne Fund Studies, 16
Peterson, Richard A., 25
PG-13-rated movies, 143
Physical violence, 86
Plato (Greek philosopher), 16
Poetics and *Politics* (Aristotle), 16
Poitier, Sidney, 59
Pokemon (video game), 125
Pong! (video game), 124
Popper, Karl, 96
Porn addiction, 109–111
Porter, Paul, 33
Potter, W. James, 76
Prevention Research Center of the Pacific Institute for Research and Evaluation, 30
Prevention Science (magazine), 89
Production Code Administration (PCA), 46–48, 144, 152

Property crime, 28
Punk rock, 24

R

R&B music, 25
Racial concerns in rap music, 27–29
Racial groups' music preference, 25–26
Radiological Society of North America (RSNA), 113
Rand, Ayn, 122
Ransbottom, Nicholas, 158–159
Rape concerns, 43–44
Rap music
    academic achievement and, 38–39
    delinquent behavior and, 38
    does not cause violence, 36–41
    effects of, 22–23
    in everyday life, 23–24
    fandom, 23
    gangsta rap music, 30–31, 38
    misogyny and, 37–38
    mood and, 39
    overview, 21, 36–37
    popularity of, 25–27
    racial concerns, 27–29
    unfairly maligned, 39–40
    violence concerns over, 30–31
Reagan, Ronald, 17
Realistic violence, 154
Rebel Without a Cause (film), 65
Red Dead Redemption (video game), 124
Renshaw, Perry F., 106–107
The Republic (Plato), 16
Reward or punishment and violence, 151–152

Richie, Nicole, 141
Rihanna (pop singer), 33–34, 42–44
Robinson, Matthew, 30–32
Rooney, Frank, 49
Ross, Dorothea, 75
Ross, Sheila A., 75
R-rated movies, 90–91

S

Sargent, James D., 89–90
Scharrer, Erica, 76, 77
Schary, Dore, 56
Schramm, Wilbur, 16
Schumach, Murray, 60
Self-destructive behavior, 22
Self-perception, 87
Sesame Street (TV show), 101
Sexual promiscuity, 38
Shepherd, Rupert, 113–115
Shurlock, Geoffrey, 47, 55, 57–60
Slate (e-zine), 18–19
Social protest in music, 24
Society for Prevention Research, 89–91
Socioeconomic status (SES), 26
Soul music, 25
Sparks, G. G., 96
Spielberg, Steven, 159
StarCraft (video game), 110
Stevens, Dana, 18–19
StrangleFest Death Party (video game), 123
Street crime depiction, 49–56
Super Bowl advertising, 79–82
Super Mario Bros. (video game), 106
Swaminathan, Nikhil, 92–94

T

Tanner, Julian, 21–29, 36
Taxi Driver (film), 17
Telecommunications Act (1985), 139
Television in the Lives of Our Children (Schramm, Lyle, Parker), 16–17
Television violence
    in advertising, 75–82
    aggressive behavior, 70–74, 84–86
    hazards of, 119
    impact of, 71–72, 118
    overview, 70, 72–74
    parental concern over, 136–137
    parental monitoring of, 135–138
    television positive vs. negative aspects, 70–71
    trauma and fear over, 74
    V-Chip device, 139, 140
Three-Hour Rule, 139, 140
Timmer, Joel, 144–157
Transformers (film), 143
Trauma from television violence, 74
Tremblay, Richard, 92–93
Trevelyan, John, 54

U

United Church of Christ, 141
United Kingdom (UK), 24
University of Chicago, 94
University of Michigan, 73
University of Montreal, 92
University of Toronto, 101

Urban Music Enthusiasts, 25–29

US Supreme Court, 103, 113, 121

V

Variety (magazine), 52

V-Chip device, 139, 140

Venice Film Festival, 65

Vick, Michael, 125

Video game violence
 addiction in males, 109–112
 aggression and, 84, 86–88
 dubious perils of, 119–121
 educational aspect of games, 107–108
 examples of, 122–125
 funding sources and, 127–129
 impact on male brain, 113–115
 influence on children, 116–118
 neuroscience of, 108
 overview, 106–108
 research on, 17, 126–129

Vizzard, Jack, 50–51

W

Walker, John, 126–129

Wang, Yang, 113–114, 127

Warren, Ron, 76

Watkins, Arthur, 53–54

Weapons, in films, 149–150

Whites, 26

Wii games, 106

The Wild One (film), 46, 49, 52–56, 59–60

Wiley, Alexander, 64

Wilson, Barbara J., 145–146, 148–149, 154

Wittgenstein, Ludwig, 95

World of Warcraft (video game), 110

Wortley, Scot, 21–29

X

X rating for movies, 48

Xanga website, 142

Z

Zimbardo, Philip G., 109–112

Zurawik, David, 18